SOUL SONGS

Cathy-
You are an
inspiration to
all who know
you. May love
always prevail
in your life.
Love,
Heidi

SOUL SONGS

REFLECTIONS OF JOY IN EVERYDAY LIFE

HEIDI LEVAN

LANGDON STREET PRESS, MINNEAPOLIS

Langdon Street Press
212 3rd Avenue North, Suite 290
Minneapolis, MN 55401
612.455.2293
www.langdonstreetpress.com

ISBN-13: 978-1-938296-10-9
LCCN: 2012947461

Distributed by Itasca Books

Illustrations by Logan Levan
Cover Design by Sophie Chi
Typeset by Mary Kristin Ross

Printed in the United States of America

LANGDON
STREET
PRESS

DEDICATION

This book is dedicated to my husband, David.
Without his ever-present love, support, and encouragement,
this book would still be only a dream.

ACKNOWLEDGMENTS

I would like to thank my son, Logan, for illustrating this book and sharing his talent. I would also like to thank my daughter, Amy, and her delightful family for inspiring me on a daily basis.

Thank you to all my friends who were part of my *Chronicles* e-mail group over the last few years. Your response to my writing has awed and humbled me so many times.

I would like to express my deep gratitude to my editor, Kate, for her thoughtful, insightful feedback and guidance. Her contributions were invaluable.

To the universe—thank you for the words, and for carrying these words to anyone who may find comfort and joy in them.

CONTENTS

Autumn

Winter

SOUL SONGS

Spring

INTRODUCTION

To dance amidst the mundane routines and responsibilities of everyday life has long been my quest. For many years I have studied the books, thoughts, and actions of great spiritual leaders, observing life with a desire to achieve a higher level of living. Many of the leaders I found fascinating traveled to faraway places or spent months alone to arrive at that higher understanding. With a home, husband, children, elderly parents, a career, and a mortgage, those were not viable options for me. Through it all I kept saying, "You have to aspire to this spiritual, peaceful understanding simply by living everyday life." I believed there was a way to live with enlightenment and find the song of my soul without turning everything upside down. There had to be or I was toast!

I began a journey—a journey to find magic in the common world around me and a journey to find my own joy and spiritual deepening within me. Along the way, I began to write my observations on this path—the joys, the lessons, the sadness, the stillness, the action, the sweetness, and the soulfulness of life. My discovery was simply that all around us, wherever we are, we have daily opportunities to be alive. Our movement through life is the joy, the fascination, the magic, the knowing. *We* are the joy in everyday life.

Long ago I realized that sharing who I was—my heart

and soul—brought me closer to others and to myself. While this book is my journey, my deepest hope is that it will inspire you to smile more, laugh more, dream more, love more, and find your own joy in the world around you.

Soul Songs is a compilation of what I refer to as my "ponderings." May they spark your curiosity and passion for finding your own soul song through the joy in everyday life.

SUMMER

BIG WISHES

In a magical corner of the far field, the giant puffballs grow. Dandelion puffballs pale in comparison to *these* puffball wonders. They are so large that their seedpods look like little parachutes when they are sent to join the wind.

My grandson once declared that the big puffballs are for big wishes. I stood looking at the puffball giant, thinking of my grandson's belief, and bent down to pluck the puffball. You must be very careful when you pluck them, because their size is deceiving and they are very fragile. If a puffball spills the seedpods before you make your wish, the magic is gone.

Holding the puffball perfectly still, I closed my eyes, made a big wish, and sent a shower of seeds of positive possibilities into the world.

Puffballs are more about faith than wishes. What we believe is what is for us. When my daughter was four years old, she taught me this lesson. She came rushing into the house in late afternoon with a limp and lifeless dandelion in her little hand. "Here, Mommy," she said. "Put this in water and it will turn into a sunshine." I looked at the poor, pathetic dandelion and knew with absolute certainty that it would never be "a sunshine." But she was looking at me with such earnestness that I could not bear to tell her the truth. So, I stuck the dandelion in a little vase in the middle of the table and promptly forgot it existed.

The next morning I stumbled to the kitchen, and even in my drowsy state, I was stunned. There in the middle of the table was the dandelion. I was correct—it was not the sunshine my daughter had predicted. It was, however, a delicate, perfect puffball. I was in awe. In my ignorance, I would have simply tossed this seemingly hopeless specimen aside and never known the secret of its unique beauty and possibilities.

My daughter's faith was inspiring and has always stayed with me. Sometimes we are so ingrained in our own thoughts of how life should be that we don't see the unexpected beauty of how it might be. I often apply this to people. We are not all destined to be bright, yellow sunshine but we are all as uniquely beautiful as the delicate whisper of the puffball.

RHYTHMS

I like to watch the earth wake up. The morning sunlight has a golden hue that steals across the landscape and rests on the trees in a way that is softer, more subtle, than the rays of the day. Birds sing quieter, with just a few to warm up the chorus, and gradually the rest of the orchestra chimes in. They intuitively understand how to be still as the day awakens.

My husband does not intuitively understand how to be still as the day awakens. He turns on an abundance of bright lights, eats breakfast immediately, makes noise as though it were noon, and engages in conversation. I wake up like the earth; it is a gradual dawning. I get up earlier so I can wake up slower. Now, if my husband got up first, fed the animals and made his own breakfast (in other words, if he lived alone), *he* could control how the day begins. Since that is not the case, yours truly is the lead ray of sunshine (or not) in our house. We conserve on electricity, we do not converse in more than two words at one time, coffee is essential, and we eat breakfast primarily by candlelight. (This is not a romantic gesture.)

It took my husband a few years after we were married to grow hair back on his forearms. He kept forgetting about the candles when he reached for the salt. He has adjusted to this "waking up slow" process because he has grown to understand that *not* allowing this to happen sets a tone for the day that is not particularly enjoyable.

We create rhythms of life—routines that we take for granted. We think they are mundane and chide ourselves for being inflexible. These rituals provide us, however, with a sense of constancy that humans crave. As the pace of our world increases, these elements of constancy grow more important. We love to go on vacation but are always glad to come home because our rhythms of life are disrupted. Even people who travel a great deal create some type of routine. We can laugh at ourselves and our funny quirks, but we would be lost without them. They are our antidote to life's uncertainties.

Appreciate the rhythms you have created. These rituals preserve your sanity.

MY FATHER'S HANDS

I sat on the deck today and looked up at the absolute blue of the sky and was amazed to see diamonds everywhere. That's right—diamonds. The sun was at just the right angle to turn all the bugs to glittering diamonds and they filled the sky like daytime stars. Sometimes the most common things become diamonds in our life.

Have you ever considered the magnificence of hands? Such common instruments that yield uncommon results. My favorite of my father's features was his hands. They were short, rather stubby hands, and though he worked outside on the farm they did not have one callous. They were strong and capable hands. I look at my own and they are just the same. But how many times do we really look at our hands and consider what they represent?

Hands communicate even if we can't speak. They have powerful conversations without words. They touch someone's shoulder at just the right moment. They wipe a tear away, they applaud, they roll into tight balls when we are afraid or angry, they paint, they wave. Our hands allow us to write, to eat, to grasp, to caress, to hold a book or a child. They reach out, they push away, they tickle, they play music, they write words. They are simply incredible parts of ourselves that we often take for granted.

I remember my father's hands because they were

symbolic of the strength and security and love that I felt growing up in his life circle. The hard work he did each day did not toughen him or his hands. And so, thinking of his hands will always soften my heart.

Today, stop for just a moment, and look at your hands. And then touch the hands of someone you love and be grateful for the miracles of common things.

SWEET IMPERFECTION

Summer has arrived! The birds raise their voices in gratitude and joy. The sun glides unhindered by clouds across the pure blue sky, sending showers of sparkling light upon the life below. The smell of freshly cut grass and a warming earth wafts upon a breeze that barely touches the skin. Daisies wave along the roadside, and roses share their abundant beauty in the gardens. The gentle time of year.

Roses and lilies from my garden, tossed in a crystal vase, grace my coffee table. These are not the perfect roses from a florist's shop that stand straight and poised. While the perfection of purchased roses is beauty in itself, it is the softer imperfection of roses from the garden that speaks to my soul. They open widely, fill the air with sweet fragrance, and as they fade, their petals fall softly upon the earth below. Their presence is peaceful, uncontrolled.

I find the imperfection in people far more satisfying than the perfection we all strive for. It is the imperfection that allows us to flow and grow and thrive with sweetness and grace.

I believe it is not so much what we do in life, but what we learn from life that is significant. We spend so much of our time trying to be more than what we are. There is a compulsion to judge others to make ourselves feel less "lesser than." One of the things I have learned from life is to judge less. The old adage "Walk a mile in their shoes" is a wise one. It is only through compassion and empathy that we see the light in life. Through painful moments and memories, I have learned that those who judge the most, miss the most. The imperfection in all of us should compel us to step back and allow the lines of black and white to blur. All is not what it seems.

On these beautiful summer days and nights, I think about the sweetness of life. It is extraordinarily rewarding but sometimes very hard to capture a moment when the world is spinning around us with all the demands and responsibilities of living. Some days I notice the beauty, but I don't feel the beauty. And when I am in that constricted space, I find I judge others more. I am stilted by the confines of structure and accomplishment.

Today I thought about the roses from the garden and craved the opening of my heart and soul to the sweetness of the imperfection in myself, and in others. Today I will remember to allow myself a moment to be like the roses. If some of my petals fall to the ground, they will do so with grace.

BLISS

The sun was not hiding behind the skirts of the clouds this morning. It slipped silently over the horizon, spinning everything it touched to gold. The effort of man to collect and create gold was tawdry in comparison to the ease of nature with its single sweep of sunlight. For these few moments, the earth sighed with bliss.

My little grandson fell asleep in my arms riding the zoo train yesterday. This is bliss for me. It comes from deep within and absorbs every corner of you. It is joy and peace wrapped into one emotion and runs like warm wine through every fiber of your being. Bliss can be sustained, like holding a sleeping child, or it can be but a brief moment, like putting on a new pair of soft socks on a brisk autumn morning. Most of the time, we hurry through life and do not recognize—and, therefore, do not experience—the bliss that regularly surrounds each one of us.

The fascinating thing about bliss is the more you feel it, the more it appears in your life. It builds upon itself. Bliss is finding what you love to do, love to feel, love to think. I feel bliss when I hear raindrops on the leaves outside my window just before I fall asleep with a kitty curled up beside me; when I am absorbed in a project I enjoy; when I sense the smell of wood smoke, coffee, or baking bread; when I watch leaves swirl and glide on the wind; when I feel the sun warm every ounce of my body on a summer's day; when I buy books or dance with my husband. I feel bliss when the morning is young and there is a blanket to my chin; when I arrange flowers or set a perfect table; when my children and grandchildren are all under one roof.

"Follow your bliss" is a famous quote by Joseph Campbell. Bliss will lead you, moment by moment, to places of peace and contentment. Allow yourself to savor the bliss. This is a gift that lasts far longer than the moment in which it arrives.

May you recognize, and experience, one moment of bliss today. And may you experience two moments of bliss tomorrow.

FAITH AND FLOWERS

The sunshine was everywhere and I felt the heat all through my body. I was on my knees in fresh dirt. There was a hole in my glove and my fingernail caught the dirt like it used to when I was a child building roads through the weeds. I was planting flower seeds. I carefully created the little trench and crumbled fine dirt over the tiny seeds and patted them with loving faith that soon they would sprout and be beautiful testaments to the glory of nature, and life.

Do we have that kind of faith in ourselves? Do we plant the seeds and cover them with dirt, knowing they will grow and be beautiful? All we seem to see is that the seeds are so small and the dirt is so thick; we doubt our ability to grow and express beauty. We don't have faith that we will sprout through the dirt, grow in the warmth of the sun and the rain, and become beautiful testaments to the glory of life.

Like the flowers that grow from the seeds, we often find that it is difficult to sustain our beauty once it has blossomed. If we forget to water the flowers, if we forget to provide them nutrients to grow, or the sun beats too intensely and we have not provided them shade, they wilt, and sometimes they die.

As adults, we forget to care for our souls in the hurry of life, and when we do, we also wilt. Without a moment of shade, or a drink of water when we are depleted, or protection when the world is too intensely hot or cold, we compromise our ability to be beautiful and to share that glory of life with others.

Beauty lives within each of us. May we nurture the growing beauty today so that we might share it more fully tomorrow.

BEAN BATTLES

The house is quiet in this warm summer moment. Even the birds are quiet and the kitties are either asleep or walking softly on their pads. I love the peace. I savor the peace. With the sweet breeze moving through the windows, touching my toes and brushing my cheeks, I feel the euphoria of the finest dream in this summer morning and I remember summer days gone past.

You learn how to work growing up on a farm. My father worked swing shift on the railroad and day shift on the farm. He had many things to accomplish during that day shift and he fully expected his children to contribute to the success of the "organization," which we did. Most of the time.

In mid-summer we were sent to the garden and sentenced to pick the beans, which went on in endless rows. After a few industrious moments of picking the beans, my brother would begin to throw dirt clods at everything that moved (including me) and the bean rows became his battlefield. I would sit in the row and make pictures on my shirt out of the bean leaves that stuck to me as though I were a felt board. After a while we'd bury ourselves in the dirt and unbury ourselves by pretending we were shaving our legs with sticks. Oh, we were very creative—until we heard Dad coming.

Now, I am quite certain that my father knew what we were really doing and that he did not have unrealistic expectations of how many beans we were going to pick or how fast we were going to pick them. I think he really just wanted some peace and quiet and knew we'd be out of his way if he ordered us to the garden. Pretty smart guy, my father!

Sometimes you need to remember where you began to figure out where you want to go —for example, the things you loved to do as a child. We spend too much time thinking about the things we don't love instead of the things we do love. My father always described me as being very positive—I knew positively what I did and did not want to do. Well, I think we are all that way as children and then there is this responsibility thing that arrives and we become less and less positive about what we do and do not want to do. We shove it down deeper and deeper until it becomes like a buried treasure and we can't recall quite where we put the map that would help us discover it again.

We often hear aging described as a curse, but, at least at this point in life, I think it has some positives. Often, you have the opportunity to find that buried treasure chest filled with the things you love and want to do again. Sometimes the treasure arrives even before you have the freedom to explore it with abandon, but when it arrives, you know it, and you begin the journey back regardless of where you are in life. You have found the map. It looks a little foreign now, but with every step it will make more sense and you will wonder how you could have strayed so far from the little being you were when you started this life journey.

The first step may be remembering what you loved to do as a child. The remembering itself will allow you to uncover treasures that will make you laugh, and love, and dance more every day.

Remember one thing today that you used to love to do when you were very young. By doing so, you have just found your treasure map. May your journey bring you many moments of joy.

BARE FEET

It was the hottest of summer days. The heat hung over the land. Even the cats stretched long to gain relief. As evening promised its arrival, I slipped off my shoes and sat on the front steps. The breeze that had begun to whisper very quietly in the trees did not reach me there. I ventured higher to the swing in the upper yard. It was not my intent to go that far with my bare feet hollering about the textures and potential thistles and sticks they might encounter. Even there the breeze did not reach. Apologizing to my feet, I sought even higher ground. The highest point of hilltop paradise—the garden. No thistles and no snakes. So far.

On hot summer evenings, we can always count on a caressing northwest breeze slipping over the garden, and this evening was no exception. I sat on the garden tractor and watched my husband watering his grapes, with the warm, soft wind sliding over my skin. There was not a cloud in the endless blue sky. The swallows were dipping and diving and cavorting across the blue, oblivious to the heat of the day. They were not the only birds playing with the breeze—others darted in and out of the trees surrounding the garden. There was no sound but an occasional rustling of leaves and the cheerful chatter of the birds.

I sat there, absorbing the beauty that greeted me at every

angle. My feet still tingled from the coolness of the grass. I could smell the ground absorbing the water my husband was generously distributing. The sky turned to hues that artists will never succeed in capturing as the sun gracefully retreated beyond the hills. I could almost hear the earth sigh with relief after such a hot day.

I sat there until the first star appeared in the sky. I thought about how much change the past year had brought me and yet how much it all stays the same. I walked back to the house, my feet reveling in the cool grass. I knew I lived in paradise and I was grateful that this hottest of summer days had not passed me by without a deep appreciation for the moment.

JAMMING

Clouds are hanging low this early summer day carrying dampness to the abundant leaves of the strawberries and young garden plants. The smell of moisture wafts along the newly turned ground, freshly mown grass, and silently swaying maple leaves. Soon the rays of the sun will slip through the mist and dry the earth—the ever-present balance for thriving.

Today I made freezer jam. Making jam and canning sauerkraut are remnants of a former life. I began canning and freezing the summer before my husband and I were married. I had been so into this domestic scene that I even drew little hearts on the tops of the lids.

Jump forward about ten years. I was now the mother of two little children, working, and applauding myself when I could put one foot in front of the other at the end of the day. My husband was planting a huge garden and proudly bringing in buckets of produce . . . for me to can and freeze. I would look at those buckets and want to cry. If I complained about it, he would pout and mutter, "I don't know why I even plant a garden!" And I would reply, "I don't know why you plant a garden for an army!" The conversation would go downhill from there.

In order to regain wedded bliss, I started throwing half

of all the produce he brought home over the hill while he was at work. (You can do that when you live in the country.) Now I had a more manageable workload and he didn't know what I had done. (This is called a "solution-oriented marriage strategy.") Since that time, my husband has revised his expectations for my canning and freezing achievements but he still plants a big garden. He has tried to explain to me, without success, on *several* occasions, that you can't plant two tomato plants, you have to plant ten. I simply shut my mouth and hope the birds like tomatoes!

They say compromise is the key to a happy relationship. I think a little creativity is also required.

FADED BLUE

On a glorious summer morning, even though the sun was just beginning to wash across the sky, the wind was warm as it breathed across my skin, rustling the leaves and muffling the sound of my steps on the dusty gravel road. The sky was cloudless, an expansive mass of faded blue reminding me of infinity and possibilities. The day would be beyond warm, but for now, it was paradise. May this moment, on this beautiful summer day, remain in my memory forever.

We live in a restrictive state much of the time where true appreciation for the infinite and possible is rarely given the time to settle in our minds. While infinity is an enchanting concept, it can also be overwhelming in a world that is bound by time. We push against life by trying to control it, forcing it to fit in our ways.

I have recently stopped wearing a watch except when I absolutely need one. When I do wear one, it is heavy and binding on my wrist. I notice it now where I had grown accustomed to it before. It is symbolic of how we become embroiled in the ways of human expectations and become lost in the "Can't do" rather than the "Can do." If we dare to explore the possibilities, almost in the same breath there is a list of impossibilities to stop us in our thoughtful tracks. The fascination in this is how we convert what we intuitively know about the power of potential and positivity in our life to the reality of the places and spaces we live in. Triumph would be learning how to do this. I capture it in rare moments but it is heady enough that I must continue to strive for this.

The wind tossing to and fro today is the epitome of the flow of the universe. The wind touches everything and is nothing. When I consciously try to be more like the free-spirited, ever-moving wind, I feel the ease of life pour over me.

PAPERCLIPS

The sweet smell of the big cottonwood tree in the dip of the road drifted across the field and surrounded me. The screech of a red-tailed hawk as it glided effortlessly on the breeze was the only sound that permeated the heat of the day. One lonely wisp of cloud pirouetted across the pale blue sky. It was an easy afternoon. An afternoon for an easy task.

Today I cleaned the junk drawer. I thought once the kids moved out we would always have a clean, organized junk drawer. Not true. I am occasionally forced to clean the drawer when it will no longer open.

How do we acquire so much junk? I don't remember consciously deciding to obtain it but somehow we collect an abundance of it until it all gets jumbled together and we can't tell a rubber band from a paperclip. Paperclips—a means to control chaos. I tossed the flimsy, plastic ones, the bent ones that were no longer able to control anything. I kept the standard, useful ones and a few larger ones for projects needing more control. Then I pondered over why I had so many of those big, honkin' ones that are more like clamps than paperclips. Is that not just a little like the control mechanisms we create for ourselves in life? Do we not need to occasionally sort them and rid ourselves of the flimsy, broken ones, keep the ones that serve us well, and ponder deeply if we have too many of the big, honkin' ones? What can we let go, toss away, disregard? What no longer fits? Do we keep them because we needed them once and are afraid we might need them again?

Junk drawers contain all kinds of things: staplers to hold things together and staple pullers to take them apart when we make a mistake; scissors to cut away and tape to hold back together; glue to stick together and tacks to hold things up; more pencils and pens and markers than an overflowing tray can hold. In our life we are constantly sorting through our own "junk drawers" of "tools" we have collected to cut away, hold together, stay up, stick together, speak up, and shut up, along with quite a few things we just hang on to because we might need them, someday. This arsenal of defenses gets all tangled up until we can't tell if our life is ours or just something we borrowed from someone else.

What are you keeping in your junk drawer that no longer has any value? What has you tangled to the point where you do not have room to take in something wonderful because you are holding on to something that is . . . well, junk? The junk drawer in your home is much easier to sort than the junk drawer of life.

SECRET SANDWICHES

The air surrounds the world with the softness of a blanket.
Wild honeysuckle display their subtle orange and red finery
from the depths of the green forest; the thimble berries
bloom profusely amongst the fully developed fronds of the
ferns. The honeybees swarm amongst the blossoms of the
raspberries; the summer birds alternate between singing their
opera and feeding themselves and their babies. The candles
of new growth on the fir trees have simply become The
Tree; the flowering trees are now simply The Tree. Instead
of individual outstanding displays of color, there is a blend
of beauty that signifies that we are in the midst of summer.
There is roundness to this season—all-encompassing warm
breezes that rustle the abundance of life—a time of caressing.

I had the most phenomenal lunch today. My guests
were two very handsome, winsome little boys. We started
with an appetizer, wild blackberries picked fresh from the
vine leaving purple stains on our hands and shirts. Then we
made our way to the small fort alongside the road. The limb
shaped as a Y marks the path and we picked our way over the
obstacles before carefully placing our blanket over the dried
ferns and branches. Our fare consisted of "secret sandwiches"
(brown sugar sandwiches—Grandma's favorite, but don't tell
their mother!) and special juice (sparkling cider) and chips.

We sat amongst the swaying limbs of the trees with the sweet summer air tossing our hair and we laughed and ate. It was a divine moment of heaven for me, a cherished moment to recall during the long days of winter ahead, and beyond.

The visits of my grandchildren are designated days when I can forget about accomplishing anything and simply relish their smiles and their presence. I live in the moment and love every moment. Every other day, no matter if I work part-time, full-time, or no time at all, is filled with "doing things" and so I'm never "done." I am a master at creating inner tension with lists of things to do. I'm up to my eyeballs on a daily basis. How do I stop?

When we traveled to the Virgin Islands, we went on a submarine that dropped eighty feet under the sea. As we descended below the surface, I grew very still. Not out of fear or because of the beautiful fish or plant life but because I was in awe of a world that does not exist for us until we dip below the surface. It truly is a whole new world and I was spellbound. Life below the surface is teeming with activity and busyness. And so I wondered if the purpose of life on this planet is activity and little rest. I had believed that learning to be still and appreciate life should take a much higher precedence for us. I still believe it. Only now I wonder if the nature of humankind is centered on movement and the lesson is simply to find the balance.

For me, this balance is learned through eating secret sandwiches with little boys....

REFRESH BUTTON

It rained yesterday. As I walked this morning, the air felt newer. The road was still damp in places and the sunlight glancing off the trees turned their leaves to a richer hue. All the earth seemed to be breathing more freely and deeply, refreshed from the gift of a rain shower amidst the dry days of summer.

As we scurry through our days we can easily end up like the parched earth of summer unless we take the time to give ourselves the gift of refreshment. It takes courage to do this because it is not an easy task to accomplish. Anyone who has accumulated more than a year's worth of vacation time is in desperate need of a day of refreshment. I have long believed that personal time makes people more focused and positive and should be required by employers as a strategy for productivity and retention. Even those who are not part of the traditional workforce find their lives filled with obligations and activities until the clarity and peace of life disappear. We are masters at creating inner tension. We are taught to give until we are depleted, until our personal power and professional contributions are diminished.

Even the analytical technology of computers has a refresh button. Sometimes our computers become so clogged that the refresh button doesn't work and we have to shut the power off and give the computer a few seconds to rest before we turn it back on. Many times, taking that simple break will reset the computer's brain and efficiency. We may need to do the same.

Hitting your own refresh button means taking a day for you. It doesn't mean a day to clean the gutters, do the grocery shopping, go to the dentist, visit elderly relatives, take the dog to the vet, or mow the lawn. It means doing what you want to do that day, with or without others. For instance, every year my husband goes hunting for a week. This is his refresh time—his escape from the routines and responsibilities of life (and from his wife). Hunting energizes and recharges his internal batteries, and he returns with his operating systems restored.

Find a day for you to hit your refresh button. Plan the day, add it in indelible ink to your calendar, and make sure it happens. That simple rain shower amidst the heat of life will make an amazing difference.

TOILET PAPER TOWERS

An incredible ruckus began as I walked toward the garden. I am accustomed to the cheery twittering of the birds, but this was mega twittering!

Sitting on the fence were four baby swallows, still fuzzy, looking very much like tightrope walkers finding their balance on that thin wire line. Whether in fear or exhilaration of being out of the nest, they were chattering away. Their parents were swooping about, equally vocal, and would land beside one group of two and twitter and then move to the other group of two and twitter some more, coaching and encouraging and praising them to find their wings and fly from the nest. One little one was still cheeping from the opening of the birdhouse and his parents flew there to help him find the courage to take that leap. In watching this scene, I wondered if those parents felt as nervous, as protective, and as excited as humans when their babies leave the nest for the very first time. And, I wondered if there was a sense of relief when they had completed their task and had only to swoop at the bugs in the air to feed themselves. Parenting, for any species, is not an easy task.

This level of parenting energy is no longer required (most of the time) for my own children, but I am reminded of it when my grandsons come to visit. Multitasking is not a skill that lives only in the workplace! After a day on the farm, these little boys have intricately designed dirt tattoos from tip to toe. Before putting on their pj's, they end up in the bathtub. Taking a bath at Grandma's is a favorite activity, and Grandma is commanded to be in the bathroom during the "pool party." Who else is going to taste the porridge and save the boat? After a while, the youngest decides he's had enough and out he hops, bare as can be, to build a toilet paper tower. So, there I am, sitting on the toilet seat, trying to keep up with the bubble bath soup that my older grandson has so skillfully made, and encouraging the little one to build his tower higher—all the while hoping I can catch it if the tower falls toward the bathtub. Soggy rolls of toilet paper would certainly dampen the mood.

Not only are you expected to sample the soup and help build the tower, but you have to *talk* at the same time to keep the party going. But you do it because you love it, and their eyes shine brightly with delight. These are the moments you live for.

These are also the moments that make you grateful after you wave good-bye and return to your house and hear . . . nothing.

HUMAN CREATURES

From my deck I can watch nature's creatures. They are all so different, yet they live in harmony. Today I thought about each one's unique characteristics and how they relate to the same characteristics we find in people.

The butterfly is exquisite and flits and floats about, beautiful but never landing long enough to hold a conversation. The swallows' iridescent wings shimmer and shine as they dive agilely about, efficient and driven but not much fun. The squirrels chatter and chase each other as they fight over peanuts, social but dramatic about everything. The mosquitoes buzz in our ear; we strike out at them but usually end up hurting ourselves. The hawks soar higher when the crows harass them, rising above and only on occasion voicing their opinion. The rabbits hop and dash about and are very prolific—draw your own analogy on *that* one. The woodpeckers peck until they find what they need, persistently stay on the topic even when it's dead wood. Hummingbirds zip past at lightning speed to find sugar water, racing through life searching for sweetness. The cats lounge gracefully on the deck, waiting for life to surprise them, easygoing and laid back but rather unengaged. The obnoxiously loud blue jays, in their flashy bright blue coats, mimic the calls of other birds, pretending to be something they are not. The deer step elegantly from the woods and bound away like a movie in slow motion, gracious and soulful, leaving you in awe. With few exceptions, each of these creatures approaches life differently with the purpose of sustaining life for themselves and their offspring, each just trying to make it in their own way.

I think our mistake is that we view humans as one creature that should look and act the same when we are many unique creatures just trying to make it in our own way. If we accept humanity's creatures as we accept nature's creatures, we, too, might find harmony.

SUMMER SNOW

Today it snowed. Summer snow. Drifting across the air and settling on the curbs and grass with feathery persistence: cottonwood snow, as beautiful as any winter snowflake but with a carefree flight, lazier than the frozen flakes and far less hazardous to drive in.

For most of my life I have battled with what my father dubbed as "being sturdy." I have found far less complimentary names for this. And, I have purchased, if stacked on top of one another, several feet of diet books in my time. I have tried it all—all protein, no protein, low carb, protein shakes, the programs where you just eat the "special" food, hypnosis, and on and on. I wonder sometimes if we are genetically predisposed to roundness or if, because we started believing we were round, we simply stayed that way. We spend billions of dollars trying to change ourselves and it is truly puzzling to me why our weight is such an obsession. Cats don't care about this. Let me explain.

All four of the cats I will describe eat about the same amount of food, and all four sleep about twenty hours a day.

- Molly: Petite and fine-boned; mellow and sweet in disposition
- Athena: Also small but square—built like a brick—as wide as she is tall; always menopawsal

- Super: Big paws (fewer brains), large-boned, solid, big head; loves everyone and everything, brings his catches in alive
- Zeus: Long, long cat and very lean, all muscle; exceptionally intelligent with a license to kill; highest-ranking feline

Now, they have always had these same qualities; they have never changed in size. They don't seem to care about this at all. Their happiness in life is not based on size, and the cats with the most "authority" are not the ones who are happiest. The smarter and higher in authority they are, the less life seems to satisfy them. Their body size does not enter into their happiness equation at all and they do not spend time trying to change it.

Why do we?

THE CALLING

We will long for these summer nights when the rains and the icy winds haunt us in the middle of winter and all through the spring. There is a hushed stillness and silky warmth that dominate late August nights, as though the earth is taking a breath. I love these nights and try to stop long enough to acknowledge they exist. There are small signs that a change in the seasons is edging near. I don't want to miss the opportunity to capture the summer bliss—to enjoy this summer ride.

I recently attended an event where Steve Gilliland, author of *Enjoy the Ride*, was the keynote speaker. Of all the words he spoke, there was one sentence that hung in the air and stayed in my memory: "There are jobs, careers, and callings." A calling tugs at your heart—it captivates and compels us. When we are living our calling, we know it deep within and it is our song. Sometimes we really cannot explain why we are continually drawn to our calling. It isn't always what we think we want. Our heart decides differently and in a glimpse of a moment we know that we must follow it to the end, no matter where that might lead.

Callings are about listening and not about questioning. Sometimes we think callings are reserved for legends and heroes. Callings are for all of us. When your heart and soul are engaged and you feel the joy slip through you, you are doing exactly what you should be doing. It doesn't have to be grand, or artistic, or noticed. Callings can be a part of everyday life, work, or play. They are simply the "knowing" that you are living life as your soul intends.

I lament at times that I leave nothing behind for my children and grandchildren but words. My father created beautiful pieces of pottery and bronze, my mother left gifts of stitchery, and my husband crafts wood as though it were clay. These are tangible objects that will grace the homes of those who follow. Words seem like untouchable wisps in comparison, yet it is part of my calling to share with others my thoughts so that they might feel warm and welcome in a world that often feels the opposite. When my thoughts become words, my soul sings.

May you listen to your calling and find your song.

BLACKBERRY PIE

The trees stand tall outside my window, so tall they seem to catch the clouds. Their massive trunks and long, arching branches stand watch over all the creatures and foliage of the forest. When I was a little girl I would walk among the tall firs and talk to them. I picked flowers beneath their boughs, followed the paths and trails of the animals, and sat in the softness of their fallen needles. I always felt safe and protected. I still find sweet serenity and grace in their presence.

Sitting at the computer in my jeans, barefoot, with the early morning air slipping through the open window, brings me a feeling of peace and tranquility. The bustling, busy world is far beyond this place and I can think, and be, with clarity.

I believe we forget, in our fast-paced lives, to "live" the seasons outside. It is growing to be late August. The cricket conventions have begun and the shooting stars are abundant; the grass is brown and crunchy beneath our feet. The sky is a washed-out blue and the sun is beginning to slip down earlier and rise later; the harvest moons are nearly upon us. The blackberries are actually serve a purpose.

Blackberries, in the Northwest anyway, are like weeds. They will grow just about anywhere, in anything, thrive on abuse, and take great delight in annoying landowners with their persistence and prolific abilities. However, even this obnoxious species has a few redeeming qualities. In early summer the plants produce delicate pink blossoms. In August, they produce wonderfully sweet berries that we risk life and shredded limb to procure. So, in the spirit of the season, I baked a blackberry pie today.

Now, you must understand that pies and I are not bound by kinship. I have tried almost my entire life to master the art of pies because they are my husband's favorite dessert.

I am here to tell you there is no such thing as a "no fail" or "easy" pie crust recipe. That is a myth created by those who do not understand the hardship of "failing with flour." (Or is it "flailing with flour"?) I do understand the hardship. I follow those recipes to the letter: I use the vinegar or I use ice water or I don't touch it much or I touch it a lot—whatever the recipe says. Nope. I roll it out and it rips. Or it just rolls right around with the rolling pin and I have to peel it off and start over. More flour, I think. I mend the snags, cut out the crust, get it in the pie plate, and it's lopsided. I crunch the edges with a fork or I make those nifty edges with my finger; both ways it looks like a mutant crust. Never mind. It will be fine. And, I don't give a rip. But I do. Because I want it to look like the pictures and it never does. And my kitchen, my arms, my jeans, my feet . . . It looks like a flour dust storm has just hit. I slip around on the floor in my socks for days afterward finding hidden pockets of flour that escaped sweeping. I do not find this a gratifying, satisfying, or fulfilling experience.

I believe it is important to know how to be a gracious loser. So I bought the crust. The pie looks great, it tastes great, and my husband will be a happy man tonight.

SPINNING WEBS

The sun was still bright and pleasant as it glided upward in the sky. The sweltering heat would come later. Amidst this heat of mid-August, there was a subtle change in nature. As the sun moved through the trees it revealed multiple orbs of spun silk hanging like masterpieces in the spider gallery of art. Little golden leaves peeked through the green of the locust trees and gathered inconspicuously on the side of the dusty gravel road. Even as the warmth of the day increased, I knew there was change in the wind.

The human species spends much time spinning webs. The spiders do a better job. The human webs are tangled, secured to insecurity, and most often they trap the spinner more than anyone else. Humans spend entire lifetimes trying to untangle the stories they spin and the webs they weave with the telling.

The spiders create delicate, perfectly symmetrical webs that allow them to accomplish their task of survival quite nicely. I suppose the webs of humans attempt to do the same thing, but lack precision or finesse. The spider's web is destroyed frequently and they simply build another. If it can't be repaired, they start over. Human webs can also be destroyed but we cling to the past web while trying to create a new one; we don't let go or are distracted and soon the web loses its ability to catch anything but the poor human. We have one leg caught in the web and the other trying to make do with half the tools we need. Maybe we need more legs?

The beauty of the spider's web is its simplicity. They don't try to outdo each other by creating more strands, more dips or curves. The only adornment comes from the sweep of nature's breath on rare dew-laden days, turning the strands of web into the finest creation of lace.

If we can find a way to live with more simplicity and less spinning, life will not be quite so sticky.

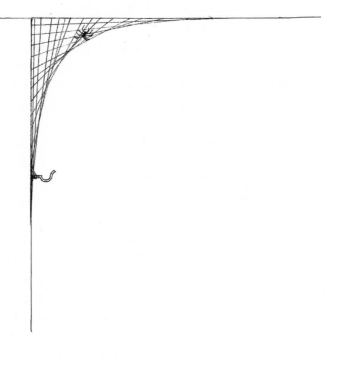

HARVEST MOON

We walked in the gathering darkness to the hilltop with the ideal vantage point for watching. There was an expectant stillness in the sweet summer air with only the sound of the crickets stirring the night. We sat in the grass and we waited for the harvest moon. A golden hue began slowly to creep across the east horizon, spreading moment by moment closer to a sphere of light that slipped silently into the sky, hanging there, suspended by invisible threads. The moonbeams melted across the landscape, turning darkness to light and creating the shadows writers have sought to describe for centuries. Huge and magical and breathtaking, the full moon of an August night.

Many times we look to nature to explain life, not for answers but for the comfort of knowing that we are as nature is. We are able to compare the flow of our life with the flow of nature. The moon is always with us. We take it for granted. We watch it move through phases, from a tiny sliver to full gallantry. It is constantly changing. So it is for us as well. Generally, the changes in life are as incrementally small as the daily changes in the moon, but they lead us to a new fullness over and over again. Change, and fullness, is not often a singular event, even though we might think it is at the time. There are days when I feel no more significant than the first sliver of the moon. There are times when I am chasing the moonbeams without ever being able to touch them, and times when they slip over me as easily as breathing. I occasionally hide in the deepening shadows, watching the light of the moon from a distance, and then one day I find I am luminescent with the fullness of a harvest moon. An ever-changing perspective, often unnoticed in the moment. The most significant changes in our lives come quietly across our landscape and shape who we are through many phases of darkness and light.

Walk to the highest vantage point and let the moonbeams find you, and remind you, that every day is a step towards a new fullness.

QUEEN ANNE'S LACE

Queen Anne's lace elegantly appears along the country roadsides, tucked quietly into the ashen brown of the tall grass seeds about to spill to the earth. Thistles, in all sizes and shapes, are in full bloom, their purple blossoms dotting the landscape. Soon the thistle blooms will turn to white cotton seeds floating across the land to nestle against the soil. Maple trees are abundant with seeds that will soon twirl to the ground like miniature helicopters. The vetch, once profusely green, now clings to the fences in faded brown glory, the nectar of its flowers turned to dark seedpods. In this quiet stillness of August, nature is preparing to reseed life.

We so often think of life as action. The faster we go, the more we get done; the more we can accomplish, the smarter we are, the thinner we are. It just takes more self-control and more time management and more initiative. Reminders to "Just do it" and "Get it done" and "Make it so" seem to be everywhere. As humans, we are tops in knowing how to race. We are pathetic at knowing how to be still. Delayed gratification has almost disappeared from our minds. Technology and convenience anytime, anywhere is what we have grown to expect.

Nature has no expectation of immediacy. The seeds are sown during this quiet time with absolute patience and certainty that they will sprout and thrive in another six months. They fall softly upon the soil, sometimes carried by the wind to a faraway place, sometimes simply slipping to the earth beneath them. There is no sense of action in this process. There is only a sense of faith. When we sow seeds in our lives, we expect those seeds will sprout and shout in about two weeks. And if they don't, we poke, we prod, we get frustrated, and we give up. If it isn't happening now, it isn't happening.

Perhaps we have it backwards. Perhaps we need to sow the seeds with a sense of stillness and faith. Perhaps what we need to cultivate is not more action but more stillness.

Learn to be still. Sow your seeds for life with more faith and less control. If you allow them to grow in their own time, they will flourish. If you stomp on them impatiently in frustration, they will surely perish.

BROWN SUGAR SANDWICHES

It was still a balmy day but there was an early morning chill and the hummingbirds and swallows have said their farewells. There are patches of gold amongst the green leaves and a few from the cottonwood tree have floated to the ground in clusters. A part of me wants to stay here in the warmth of summer, but autumn is my favorite season. It's coming.

Have you ever had one of those days you simply can't hold on to? Yesterday was one of those days. I started my morning at 6:30 a.m. dumping an entire cup of coffee on the kitchen floor. No sooner had I cleaned up this lovely mess than a tub of sour cream hit the deck as I was taking the milk out of the refrigerator. Later, I played 52 Envelope Pick Up when the box of envelopes tested the law of gravity. The real frosting on the cake was at dinnertime when the entire bowl of green beans slipped from my fingers and turned upside down on the floor. My husband walked in at that precise moment and casually inquired if we were eating Japanese-style that night.

I have had a couple days lately when I simply did not want to look outside the box or embrace change. I wanted to sit in my box wearing my favorite sweatshirt and jeans, eat a brown sugar sandwich for lunch, and forget about embracing anything but the kitty on my lap. These are the days when we learn the most because we are in a very humbling and vulnerable human place. These are the days when we take all we have experienced on the outside and learn from it on the inside. It is in this place, on these days, when we are in touch with our own humanity and build compassion and empathy and wisdom.

May you remember it is okay to have a day when you live inside the box—just don't put a lid on it.

SUMMER RAIN

Summer rain falls softly from the sky and patters upon the leaves with a brush of percussion that soothes the soul. Quietly it quenches the thirst of the earth and brings stillness to a lively season of life that relishes the moment to simply listen and be motionless.

The summer rain today is significant for me. For days and days I have been engulfed in the intense, analytical, process-oriented, problem-solving, labor-intensive business world. Stillness of mind and body has been most elusive. As aware as I have been of the imbalance, I have not been able to capture the magic moments of everyday life; I experience them instead in split seconds that slip through my mind like phantoms of a peaceful existence. The creative, soulful side of me has been lost amongst technology, paperwork, and work issues. I've felt starved of the free movement of life and yet I cannot touch it long enough to balance myself.

While I prefer sun in the summertime, I needed this rain today. There is something about the sound of rain that settles my soul. Slowly I felt the breath of energy fill me up once again, that golden ribbon of light that moves through us with a freedom and a peace that is essential to experiencing life with joy and love. I gave myself permission to go there to remember the wonderful things that I had noticed in split seconds during the last month and appreciate them as the flow of life intends. I wondered how I could have allowed myself to move so far from this place of stillness.

Even in my mortal busyness, I have noticed the rustle of the wind on the silver maple tree, the sun slanting across the hilltop and caressing the teeming life of summer grasses; the taste of strawberries picked fresh from the garden, the flowers spilling over the window boxes; the birds diligently and patiently feeding their young and singing with abandon in spite of the task; the smell of warm earth, the red elderberries dancing in the breeze, little boys jumping with delight at fireworks and homemade ice cream; the taste of potato salad, and cats stretching long in the afternoon sun. The season is turning lazy and I think that I should turn lazy, too.

As much as I believe that "Life is not about making it go faster" and that sometimes determination can deter us from what is really important, I have not been able to live my life that way the past several weeks. I am grateful today for the summer rain. It has reminded me of the loveliness I have been missing.

May each of you find a reminder, too, that life is about experiencing the magic in moments, not seconds. Let the magic fill your day with joy, peace, and love.

GARBAGE TRUCKS

Sunflowers are standing tall, their vibrant heads bowed as though in constant prayer, like majestic watchtowers amongst the garden plants. Their cheerful countenance is as tangible as a smile, promising nourishment for the birds that consume their seeds and for the people who absorb their confident power and warmth.

In the quiet peace of early morning, I began to listen to the sounds around me. I heard the garbage truck making its way along the road below the hill. I like the sound of the garbage truck. It means it is Wednesday and I know this without even having to think about it. I also like the sound of the washer and dryer. I fall asleep at night to the hum of the dishwasher and wake to the sound of coffee dripping into the pot. I love hearing distant chainsaws cutting wood in the fall and lawn mowers zipping in the spring. I love the sounds of birds singing, kitties purring, leaves whispering, and my husband breathing in the night.

I equate memories and emotions to the sounds I hear, like aromatherapy in some respects. I have watched as people age, how their lives become smaller when their hearing grows impaired. They feel like their brain power is diminishing when really it is only that they cannot hear and life exists in whispers translated to confusion; the sounds are white noise in the background. It is not until we go from hearing to listening that we realize how important sounds are to us.

If we remember the sounds we've heard throughout the phases of our life, we will find comfort in so many that we rarely think about. When I was very small, my father worked swing shift and I would lie in bed at night and wait to hear his footsteps on the stairs. As soon as I heard them I would fall asleep. I associated that sound with security. I think it is fascinating to contemplate sounds and our responses to these noises; we generally do not recognize their power or presence in our life.

Smells are also something we take for granted. I have long been interested in aromatherapy because I believe we associate certain aromas with wonderful times in our life. I read some books that described which aromas were supposed to create certain responses and I tried them. Mostly I discovered that the suggestions actually stink. So, I created my own aromatherapy. Which scents take me to places I want to be? Vanilla tops the list. Pumpkin spice, cinnamon, sugar cookies in the oven, baking bread, freshly mown grass in the spring and freshly cut hay in the summer, rain on dusty earth, fir boughs, wood smoke, clean sheets, roast in the Crock-Pot . . . All these scents bring back memories and sooth a weary soul.

May you recognize the importance of little things today and acknowledge with gratitude the sounds and scents of everyday life.

CUCUMBER SANDWICHES

The sun was hanging directly overhead, filtered only by the giant leaves on the maple tree that cast inconsistent shadows across the warm wood of the deck. The warmth of the air matched the warmth of my skin, and for just a moment, I drifted like the occasional cloud that skirted through the summer blue sky.

I ate a cucumber sandwich for lunch today, sitting on the deck in my corner of paradise. Cucumber sandwiches are one of those wonderfully elegant things I can only eat when I'm alone. I even put them on a crystal plate. My husband generally appreciates my penchant for finery but would look at me if I served things like this with that "Where's the beef?" question in his eyes. It's rather like my fondness for sweet-smelling soaps. He does okay with Meadow Mist or Orange Spice but struggles with smelling like Peach & Sweet Berries, Strawberry Cream, or Cucumber Melon when he steps out of the shower. He's a very tolerant man, but he has his limits.

Have you ever noticed how we always gravitate to the same chair? I have witnessed this phenomenon in meetings and I know it is almost a law at home. Every night at dinner my husband sits in "his" chair and I sit in mine. We never venture out of this routine. It's his chair and it's my chair. Only I like his better. So, when he isn't home, I sit in his. (I'm sure a psychologist would have lots of fun with that!) There is his side of the bed and my side of the bed; his chair in the living room and my corner of the couch. We each have our own space. (The cats actually own them all.)

Do you have a special spot in your house? A place that is "your space" where you relax into life and surround yourself with your things? My spot in our house is the left end of the couch. It's *mine*. *My* blanket awaits me there, *my* current books are beside me there, *my* notebook where I organize life is there, *my* pen is there, *my* cup of coffee is there. *My* stuff. I occasionally allow a kitty to share my blanket but no one else, thank you very much! And my husband has his space, also—the recliner across the room surrounded by *his* stuff: an atlas, wine books, tool catalogs, maps, and a magnifying glass (tee hee). *His* space has more piles than mine, but the concept is the same. How funny we are!

With change occurring all around us each day, it is important to allow ourselves opportunities to *not* change. Our space is a sanctuary and a familiar, comfortable, never-changing spot to sort out our life and feel safe. My husband may never understand floral soaps or why there are towels in the bathroom we can't actually use, but he does understand the need for a place of your very own. It is a place that is "soul full" and it is a sacred and necessary part of being a balanced human being.

ROSES TO REMEMBER

A summer rain slipped through during the night, leaving rose petals scattered across the damp grass. The earth seemed to be taking a deep breath of renewed air. The dust had settled momentarily and the air smelled of raindrops on the dry dirt. The song of the birds was sharper, clearer, and the garden plants were rising higher than they had in many days. Nature was sighing with pleasure.

On my first day of life, my father gave me a red rose. Thus began our relationship. Thirty-one years ago, my father passed away suddenly and unexpectedly. While I feel the impact of this loss every day, I have, over the years, grown to accept it. I used to buy a red rose every year on this day, and put it in a crystal vase as a simple reminder of all my father gave to me. In the fast pace of the last few years, I have not remembered to buy the rose. Sometimes we are so busy with our busyness that we forget when we should remember. I remembered this year. There is a single red rose in a crystal vase on my kitchen table in appreciation of my father's significant role in who I am. I have always felt honored to be his daughter.

I have something to confess: I have a second junk drawer. Only it is more like a treasure drawer, actually. My nightstand is filled with keepsakes—cards, notes, and a variety of other documents I don't know what to do with but don't want to throw away. I was looking for something in this drawer recently and found myself sitting in the middle of the bedroom going through all of these treasures. It became a journey of sorts.

In this drawer I found some very unusual things, including a book called *Tighten Your Tush*, old lists of what to wear on what day for work, a recipe for reindeer food, a picture torn from a magazine on which I had written *How I want to look when I'm 60*, and tons of cards, printed e-mails, and notes from friends and family, including a note my father had scribbled to me many years ago. One of the cards reminded me to "Live in the light and the shadows will fall behind you." Then there was one that offered sound advice from a different perspective: "Eat a bug every morning and nothing worse will happen for the rest of the day!"

Included in this drawer were a zillion little plastic sacks with a single button in each. Do you keep these crazy things, too? They come with every shirt or blouse or sweater I buy. The manufacturers usually sew extra buttons inside the bottom of the placket in men's clothing. Why is that? Is it just assumed that men would throw the button packets away and then the women would be frustrated when there were no buttons to replace the ones that disappear?

Looking through the treasure drawer was a nice journey for a quiet afternoon. A time to remember and a time to shake my head in wonderment at the things I keep—pieces of life gone by that I can hold in my hands for just a moment and keep in my heart much longer. Sometimes it is good to remember.

BALLOONS

Dawn arrives early in the summer, peeking over the hilltops with a sauntering light to wake and warm the earth. The stars fade to obscurity, the hush of the night slips away, and the daylight dance begins. Even the flowers raise their heads and open their petals to welcome the light of life. Every day is a first, filled with newness and promise.

I spent today, the first day of school, with my grandson. We are kindred spirits. We both wake up slowly, think *Sesame Street* is hilarious, and agree that macaroni and cheese is divine (even though I consume my caloric intake in two bites). We believe that midday naps are essential for happiness, appreciate books that provoke thoughtful action (like the ones with holes to stick our fingers through), find animals to be the greatest source of entertainment, and agree that balloons are one of the most wonderful inventions ever made. In fact, we made a trip to the store today with the sole purpose of buying balloons and Hostess Ding Dongs.

When I talk about balloons, I'm talking about the old-fashioned latex type. The Mylar ones are flashy and far more practical because they last longer, but the latex balloons "dance" more and their bright colors are captivating. Any time I see balloons, no matter where I am or what I'm doing, they brighten my day. There are just certain things in life that evoke these emotions. Pumpkins have the same effect on me. They might be sitting on a porch or mounded together in a grocery store parking lot—doesn't matter, I still smile. Cupcakes, too. They are just total mood brighteners.

Today was a grand grandma day. In the end, my grandson and I discovered something else we have in common. As much as we love each other, we both also love when Mommy comes home! But my sweet little grandson cried when I left and my thoughts driving home were of the balance and perspective a day with him brings to my life.

In honor of the first day of school—in honor of the wonder of childhood—buy a balloon. At the very least, eat a cupcake!

SHARP PENCILS

The stars slide into our skies earlier. The sun has changed bedtime, slipping below the horizon more quickly in a flourish of red, orange, and gold. The stillness comes sooner and the crickets sing longer. The grass is crunchy and dry beneath bare feet and the clouds are skipping faster to a journey unknown. The last days of summer.

The first days of school are upon us. Bright yellow school buses are stopping traffic, slowing down the morning commute. This delay can be frustrating but gives us time to remember when we were climbing on those buses: new pencils, notebooks, color crayons, scissors, backpacks; new socks and tennis shoes. The night before school started I could not fall asleep out of sheer excitement. I loved school. I loved learning. (My husband says he loved recess, lunch, and assemblies. Opposites do attract!)

Today I thought about those elementary school days and all the things I loved about them. For one thing, I loved books. I loved the way they smelled and the places they took me to. The library was a candy store to me and when the bookmobile came once a month, I was in heaven. (So was my mother, because I spent days in my room reading.) I remember the long, shiny wooden lunch tables and little cartons of milk; counting for my turn on the swings and ripping the hems out of my dresses because I played too rough; bulletin boards that changed with every season and big red rubber balls and alphabet banners strewn around every classroom; buying ice cream bars on Wednesdays with a dime; opening my lunch sack to see if my mom packed the best sandwich; riding home on the bus, mesmerized by the movement and the chatter; the perfection of sharp pencils. There is still nothing like a sharp pencil. The keys on my computer do not bring nearly the same satisfaction!

At school, I loved to do workbooks. In first grade, my cousin and I were in the same classroom. He hated to do workbooks. So, I did them for him. We had a fine arrangement. Only the teacher didn't think it was so fine and in the years that followed we were not allowed to be in the same classroom. Interestingly enough, I still like to do workbooks and he still doesn't. How fascinating it is that at such a young age we have penchants for the things that will captivate us for the rest of our life. We flourish when doing what we love and struggle through things we dislike, no matter how educated or mature we are. So many times we push against our natural aptitudes and strive to thrive in workbooks when we should be outside running marathons!

Today, make yourself the lunch you loved the most when you were in school—even if it includes a Twinkie or jelly that drips on your fingers. Remember pleasant things and the day will be better for the remembering. And if that doesn't work, go to recess!

PHOTOGRAPHS

The sun slants differently in early September. It flits across the dry grasses and swaying cornstalks, catching nature from an angle that reveals to all that fall is slipping closer. The sound of crickets fills the night air, which has grown more brisk than the hot August nights of past days. Apples fall from the trees for the deer that come when dusk gathers. Orange creeps upon the pumpkins lying in the sun as their leaves begin to wane. Mother Nature's subtle celebration of change.

My mother recently achieved her eightieth birthday. We celebrated this event with a family dinner that included her siblings from afar. My mom believes any more than six people is a crowd. So, fifteen was pushing the limits.

One of my favorite things to do is set the table for dinner festivities. This was no exception. I spend hours planning and creating the right table décor and then get frustrated when I have to actually cook. I used to like to cook but it no longer holds the glamour it once did. This may be caused by the simple fact I have prepared 10,000 dinners since the day I was married and it has since lost its glow. I keep waiting for the spark to rekindle but it hasn't happened yet.

All went well during my mom's celebration, with a couple of pre-dinner exceptions. Our dog weighs 100 pounds and his chin rests easily on the countertop. He is generally well behaved; however, when I left the room for a brief minute, he decided to help himself to half a layer of Mom's soon-to-be-frosted cake. He acquired several new names in a matter of seconds, which I will not repeat here. I had to bake another cake and the dog was banished to the garage for hours. The other hitch came when I discovered the circuit breaker had blown while dinner still had a half hour left in the oven. I was blessing microwaves profusely at that point. Being something of a perfectionist, I was not overly impressed with how this dinner party was going. There are days when things simply do not go well. This, it turned out, was one of them.

Part of Mom's birthday preparation involved rummaging through old pictures that would capture the essence of her years. It has been a life challenge for me to watch my mother grow older and to maintain my patience and compassion despite the changes I have found in her. These pictures reminded me that illness has taken its toll and that my mother is not the same person she was. Hints of the girl and the young woman have slipped away with time and loss. It is important for me to remember the more vibrant days that are reflected through these photos and to understand that within my mother's current constraints, she still feels as she did long ago. As difficult as it sometimes is, I shall continue to try to redefine my relationship with my mother in today's world.

A line from a Bob Seger song goes like this: "I wish I didn't know now what I didn't know then." A twist of words to describe the bliss of innocence. The knowing makes us deeper. Sometimes I'd rather be shallow.

FELINE DICTATORS

The hues of the forest have shifted. The lush greens of late spring and early summer are transforming. The undergrowth has turned to brown and dots of yellow are beginning to show. The leaves are drier and rustle rather than whisper in the winds. The smell of ripe blackberries drifts by and the gravel road is sifted with fine dust just waiting for raindrops. Mostly the days are languid but when the wind arrives, the leaves decorate the paths with a message: the glorious days of autumn are coming.

Today I carried the cat on my hilltop walk. Having followed me, he commanded that he be carried the rest of the trip. So, lugging my twelve-pound feline, I made my way along the route that has become my daily routine. He remained the entire trip, lounging in my arms as though it were perfectly correct for the human to carry him about the terrain.

Zeus is without a doubt the true definition of feline royalty. He nonchalantly follows us to whatever room we happen to be in—not to be confused with needing us, he simply wants us at the ready should he desire something. Our reward is that Zeus is the most affectionate cat in the world when he chooses to be and there is no smile, except perhaps that of a child, sweeter than his. He warms our hearts and brings laughter and love to each day.

I do not believe that Zeus demands to be carried just for the ride from a human. Surely that is part of the game, but because he is so intelligent, I believe he wants to view the world from a higher vantage point. How different things must appear to him in my arms than from the ground level. (Make no mistake, Zeus would surely say, the only thing elevated about humans is our physical stature.) I'm quite certain that we would interpret the world differently if we moved along on our stomachs. A different perspective opens up an entirely different window. How differently we might think if we truly did walk in the shoes of others.

Try to observe life from a different perspective today. Or, just carry a willing cat for a while. If nothing else, it will remind you how you would feel if you gained twelve pounds!

SEPTEMBER CROCUS

September has arrived with cloudy skies, moments of sunshine, and much cooler temperatures. The sun sets much earlier now and opportunities to sit on the deck in the evening have slipped away. Amidst the shifting, subdued colors of nature, there arises the September crocus. That's right, the crocus! They poke their delicate lavender heads up through the dry, brown earth in deep contrast to the rest of the hues we see this time of year. This just proves that even in nature there are elements of defiance. I can relate!

It is absolutely fascinating to me that bulbs and flowers know when to bloom. Daffodils bloom in the spring, daisies and dahlias bloom in the summer, and autumn crocuses bloom in September. How do they know to do this? How do we know when to bloom? I'm sure science explains how flowers know when to bloom, but what about us? I do not believe our DNA is programmed so that we intuitively and flawlessly bloom at a certain time in our life. How do we know when to make our dreams come true, kick up our heels, or glow with the vibrancy of life?

There is a line from a song in *Pinocchio* that says, "If your heart is in your dream, no request is too extreme." I believe that is true. Even as a young child I recognized this. When my heart was deeply engaged in a dream, the dream came true. And when I was disappointed because a dream did *not* happen, I understood that it wasn't what I really wanted deep within. I wasn't engaged in the wanting. The hard part has always been deciphering the dreams of my heart and the dreams that are inadvertently created by the circumstances surrounding me.

Perhaps we have been blessed with something that nature has not: the gift of blooming whenever our heart desires. Taking the time to listen to our heart then becomes an essential part of making our dreams come true.

I am inspired by the rebellious September crocus. It reminds me that we can bloom whenever we want, wherever we want. I'm thinking today would be a good day to bloom.

BLANKETS

It is a perfect Indian summer morning. The air is cool, brushing the parched earth with a gentle caress. Small birds are twittering the notes of a remembered summer song and the sky is a sleepy blue. The sweetness of the early hour slips through the windows with a promise that the heat of the day will fade into the coolness of night once again. When the winter winds blow, I will remember this morning with its promise that another morning just like this one will return again.

Blankets are little gifts from heaven. They protect us from the coldness we find in this world, whether physical or emotional. We hide there, we conspire there, we rest there, we are safe beneath the soft folds of these gifts. No one can touch us under the blanket.

Children understand the value of blankets. Many would like to take their blankets with them wherever they go. It might be a better place if we all had one to take with us into the world! How much healing power a simple blanket can have. Just holding one in our arms lowers our anxiety level. After a particularly challenging day—when you should have never gotten out from under the blankets in the first place—it is truly blissful to curl up under a blanket and let the tension slide out through your toes. Warm, soft, protective. All that has been in the day ceases to be.

We all have a need for protection, for safe places. There are people in my life who mimic blankets. They provide me with warmth, acceptance, a feeling of calm and peace. They are people who are able to wrap their energy around me and revive the inner core of who I am. It is not what they say, or what they do, but who they are and how they perceive life. They carry with them a loving countenance. Gifts from heaven.

CLOUD WALKING

I was walking in the clouds this morning—literally. The clouds had settled softly upon the hilltop and the mist was clinging to my skin. Every cobweb and each blade of low-lying grass were turned opaque by the dew. What once was nearly invisible was now revealed. My world was enveloped in oneness with the clouds we most often view from afar.

Walking through the clouds this morning made me think about how we walk through life. Often we view life from a distance but truly only experience it when we are one with it. So many adventures unfold before our eyes and yet they don't hold a sense of reality. Sometimes we create this unreality so we can survive difficult times and hectic days. We rob ourselves of the ability to truly experience life.

I have just gone through a time when work so consumed me that everything else slipped to that place of unreality, and I could not experience all the things I knew I should be experiencing. The universe was trying to remind me that I needed to go back; during a presentation, one line struck me: "Time is finite and our need for it is infinite." How true! Only humans create a bondage to time. Nature does not move according to a clock but by an internal evolution that takes it to the next step. The only deadline nature lives by is the next moment that takes it to the next moment. How had

I allowed time to dominate my life so much that I could not even remember what mist on my cheeks felt like, much less appreciate the wonder of it all?

So, I made a conscious decision to move back to where I longed to be. I used time to my advantage. I used time to find my path to a peaceful place. Every day I wrote something, anything, just to take me to the creative side of who I truly am. I played the piano, I walked, I sat still and did nothing but listen to my heart instead of my head. I took a nap, I picked flowers, I lay on the grass in the dark of the night and looked at the stars. I watered my flowers and ate cherry tomatoes from the garden. I bought new candles and lit them in the middle of the day. I looked at catalogs and cleaned my closet—anything and everything I could think of to lead me back to my personal satisfaction and joy.

I am happy to say it worked. Slowly the peace and serenity of my soul could breathe again and fill the empty spaces with warmth and love and appreciation for the magic and beauty that surrounds me. I had walked through this cloud for a reason. It reminded me of what was real—that I could make a choice to return from the confines of the finite to the wondrous infinity. I am grateful today for the mist on my cheeks and the hidden treasure of the cobwebs.

AUTUMN

WHAT IFS

Nature is indecisive these days. It does not seem to want to let go of summer and yet autumn beckons and tugs at the currents of change. Some days are cool and wet, and then the next day the sun owns the sky and it is warm. Today is a little of both, cloudy but warm with high humidity and no fall breeze. There is some evidence of a changing season but few foliage deities are showing their splendor. A time of transition. A stillness in movement. Going with the flow.

Humans experience these transition times as well. We're not sure how to go forward, or when, yet we know that life will indeed move us, regardless of our uncertainty of what that might mean. Unlike nature, humans worry. We play out every scenario in our minds many times over and end up back in the same place each time: generally uncertain and with a fear of the unknown. The "what ifs" are not part of what nature is doing today. The complexity of the human species is a triumph and a detriment, depending on the day.

"Going with the flow" is an overused phrase, but if we really did what the saying suggests perhaps we would find enjoyment in the transitional days rather than concern. There is value in the quieter times when change and movement are not equal to the pace of the Indy 500. We do not always have to know what our goal is. Sometimes we just need to see where life takes us and accept that the trip is not always filled with insight and action. As long as we believe that splendor awaits, and that our "leaves" will turn and be glorious with the changes we will come to know, going with the flow can be easy on our overactive human minds.

Life is not always about being active. Sometimes it is about patience and routine and appreciation for the quiet transitions and mundane times. Enjoy the moment! These times prepare us for the swirls of the future.

TREASURES

It is a time of transition for Mother Nature. The first day of autumn is upon us and we have been splattered with raindrops, cooler temperatures, and then bursts of sunshine that tease us into believing summer is still with us. We built our first fire of the season in the fireplace. I made stew for dinner and an apple pie (I bought the crust), and purchased a new book and put up my fall decorations. The autumn wreath above my mantel winks at me with little white lights casting a brighter mood than the darkness that gathers earlier these days. The animals are more content to spend time in the company of their humans.

A nightlight in our bathroom with a tiny lampshade that twirls when the light is on from the heat of the bulb is one of my favorite treasures. The definition of treasure is "considered especially precious or valuable." We all have treasures.

I have many treasured holiday decorations. My husband often inquires if we should add on to the house to accommodate my cache. (He is very subtle.) He has a 40' x 60' shop that serves as *his* treasure chest. I rest my case. I have no more comprehension as to why the gems in his shop are classified as treasures than he has of why that nightlight is one of mine. How do our possessions become precious and valuable? It isn't their monetary value. We would never sell our true treasures. We might give them to someone who would revere them as much as we do, but to sell them would be unthinkable. So, what is it that ties us to them?

I've spent some time pondering this. My conclusion is that these treasures touch our soul, or represent our soul, in some special way—they are part of the essence of who we really are. Then I wondered how a motor or a saw in my husband's shop could be a soulful thing. So I wandered into the shop and looked around at his treasures. In one corner is hunting equipment, neatly put away. In another is the small foundry setup he inherited from my father. There is the first band saw he ever bought, his brand-new fishing boat, his 1959 Massey Ferguson tractor, and the mounted deer head that I won't allow in the house. These objects are, if I really think about it, reflections of the things he loves. (I don't care how much the mounted deer head reflects what he loves, Bambi trophies are not coming in my house!)

My treasures are slightly different, but they, too, reflect the things I love: my grandmother's china, the crystal butter dish with its elegant cover, the tiny bead that hangs from my car mirror that my son gave me during troubled times, my Demdaco Willow Tree angels, the glass lemon juicer that was my mother's, the watercolor picture my daughter painted when she was five, the red glazed pot Dad made, tiny crystal vases, and my *Dandelion Cottage* book. All gifts and treasures that tell a story about my life and represent important pieces of who I am.

This autumn season, may you find a treasure or two, a new beginning or two, and always remember to take a moment or two to notice and appreciate all that surrounds you.

MICE AND MONEY

The western sky, strewn with clouds, began to turn shades of pink, purple, and coral as the sun slid into its nightly slumber from our spot on Earth. In a matter of moments, the sky turned to a brilliant red and lingered for a short time before fading back to the subtle hues of paler beauty. Man cannot match the magnificence of nature, filled with unexpected gifts of splendor.

The unexpected gifts in our lives are often less obvious than the beauty of a spectacular sunset. For instance, imagine my surprise to find a mouse running around the bathtub. An understatement at best. Generally in circumstances such as this I run screaming from the room yelling for my husband. Well, I did run screaming from the room, only my husband . . . was gone hunting. The mouse resolved the issue out of pure fright and raced from the bathroom while I was jumping on the bed in terror; I never saw him again. Five cats in the house and a mouse in the bathtub! What's wrong with this picture?

After thirty-five years of marriage, my role and my husband's are pretty clear. I pack his lunch and do the laundry, he changes the oil in the cars and mows the lawn. He won't go out with me if I wear sweats in public, and I won't dance with him if he wears his suspenders. It works. And then he goes hunting. Most of the time I'm quite content to have the house to myself. This year was different.

It started with the engine light coming on in my car and then my cell phone stopped working. I had a few good days and then my mother fell at her assisted living facility, resulting in an L2 compression fracture that landed her in a skilled nursing facility and landed me in the position of having to find her an adult foster care home. There was the episode with the lawn tractor when hauling garbage to the end of the road, and the little issue with the toilet. Then the dog we inherited from my mother became gravely ill and I had to make the decision to end his suffering.

And my dear husband was hunting. It felt like a very off-balance distribution of duties. He was bonding with nature and I was battling the forces of life. (Not to be dramatic or anything.)

It occurred to me then that we often wish for more money. Yet all of the things that had happened this particular week would not have been avoided had I been wealthy. It seems we often think money will bring us a smooth-sailing lifestyle and endless happiness. I missed my husband this week. It was my unexpected gift and it reminded me that I would take my blue–jean-wearing husband any day over money. Without him around to pick up the pieces of my heart when Calm, Cool, Collected Me reaches my breaking point, all the money in the world would not be enough.

So, to show him how much I love, value, and appreciate him, I went out and bought him new suspenders.

DANCING WITH ELEPHANTS

The first week of October, the skies are a brighter, clearer, colder blue. There are trees that have donned their coats of brilliant yellow and others that have let their leaves cascade down like golden snowflakes. The vines of the pumpkin patches have died away to reveal the orange globes beneath them like beads scattered from the sky. The days are shorter, wood smoke from late-evening fires has begun to drift through the air, and chain saws gathering winter wood have replaced the hum of lawn mowers. Nature is leading us to autumn.

There is much to be learned about leading in life and being led. Mostly we are encouraged to lead and we reward leaders for this ability. Leadership is an awesome ability if it is done with integrity, intelligence, and intuitive wisdom. If we all were leaders all the time in all aspects of our life, chaos would reign. In some situations, there is divine knowledge in knowing how to be led, in knowing how to let go of our need to control all aspects of our lives.

When my husband and I first learned to dance, I had to learn to let him lead. He would stop dancing, look at me, and say, "Heidi, you're leading!" I am a strong, independent person. In order for me to allow him to lead, I had to trust him. If I did not trust him, our dances would become like ballet with elephants. It didn't work. When I did trust him, dancing became a joy. I am joyful when I dance with my husband. But I must let him lead and I must graciously be led. There are other times for me to lead, but this is not one of them. I feel an incredible freedom when I step back and allow my husband to lead the dance. I can leave the "driving of life" to someone else and simply feel the music and the magic of the movement.

We, as a society, find it difficult to trust others. We are programmed to be so self-reliant that we forget how to let anyone or anything else lead us in our lives, including a higher power. Yet by not trusting, we miss the joy of the dance. The Garth Brooks' song comes to mind: "I could have missed the pain, but I'd of had to miss the dance."

HOT, SWEET COFFEE

While autumn has been slow in coming this year, the leaves are at last a glorious canvas of color and brilliance. They are warming the landscapes and deepening the hues. The sun rises far to the south and arrives on the morning scene much later but with visionary splendor—red, soft yellow, casual pink, and then bursting into liquid gold upon the clouds. Our breath is visible in the morning air and our cheeks turn rosy in the chill. Yes, autumn may be late, but it is here now.

We take so much for granted. Seeing my breath in the cold air was a reminder of this. We just keep breathing and ignore the gift of being able to do so. Generally invisible, breath does not come into our sight until a day when we struggle to breathe. In fact, we take our body for granted most of the time until a calamity strikes. It can be as simple as injuring one finger. Suddenly we find it difficult to tie our shoes! We also take the modern conveniences for granted until we no longer have them—electricity, computers, water, heat. It is only when we are without these amenities that we truly understand and appreciate them.

Gratitude. It swells from within us and fills every part of our being. It is not a list we make and repeat in an effort to acknowledge our appreciation. It is a feeling that is rich and full and almost tangible. It is an appreciation for the abundance that we find in the simplest things—things that go unnoticed as we scurry about: hot, sweet coffee; warm hands; clean sheets; soft socks; clear water; Scotch tape; toothpaste; keys; tires; mail. We forget to be grateful for warm air rising from the vents, toilets that flush, the light that flicks on at the flip of a switch, cell phones, computers, microwaves, refrigerators.

On any given day there is a smile, a gesture, a touch, a word, a song, a moment that moves us to the place of gratitude. May you find the time in your busy day ahead to remember to say thank you—from your heart—for the simple pleasures and gifts you receive today.

CRESCENT MOON

I left my house before the sun rose today. The horizon was clothed in deep, dark hues highlighted by a subtle glow behind the mountain promising that sunshine would enchant us soon. Suspended just above the deep purple of the high peaks of the mountain was a sliver of an iridescent crescent moon. It was a reminder that magic lives for us in moments and this was one of them.

Today I was happy in moments I will always cherish. The sweet taste of cream and sugar in my coffee; the kiss of a kitty; my grandsons eating powdered sugar donuts, one little boy with peanut butter straight from the jar on fingers and face; rhyming games and laughter with my grandsons in the sunshine; doing the dishes for my hard-working daughter; reminding my mother of how life had been on the farm to help her smile; turning up the country gravel road after a long day; watching the sun slip low and slow from the sky and being overwhelmed with gratitude for the peace of home . . . Simple moments, moments we take for granted without appreciating how they bring us that sensation of happiness.

Happiness truly does come in moments. As I left this morning I knew the day would be long and that I would have to make decisions that I did not want to make. I thought about how some days are difficult and prayed I would find moments in this day to rekindle my soul and my faith in the magic of everyday life. I was not disappointed. Sometimes we have to look for these moments and hold them close to us and revel in the fact that on almost any given day we *can* find them—that they are there for our taking if we allow them to guide us through the rocky waters.

To say that every day of my life I am filled with peace and joy would not be realistic or honest. To say that every day I find moments of peace and moments of joy, and gratitude that these moments exist, would be absolutely the truth. Tonight as the darkness gathers, I will let all the distractions perish from my thoughts and simply say thank you for the happiness in the moments of today.

I wish for every one of you the magic of a crescent moon and powdered sugar donuts.

SWEATSHIRT SLEEVES

The air was much colder today, with the dew hanging heavy on the grass, compelling me to tuck my hands inside my sweatshirt sleeves and pick up the pace of my walk. The terrain is surprisingly green for October but the chill of the still morning was filled with the knowledge that autumn is here.

I grew up on this land upon which I walk. How many times the surface of this land has changed in my lifetime. Once untended, it became the home of potatoes, strawberries, gardens, wheat, and pastureland. Trees have been planted, trees have been cleared, and trees have been planted again. Houses and barns have disappeared, and new houses and barns have been built. The land has gone through countless transformations over time, yet this is only the surface. The core of the land lies unchanged beneath.

Are we not like the land? Throughout our lives we are transforming our personal landscape, our personal surface. Over and over again we meld and mesh and move to ensure we are progressing through all the appropriate steps of a human life. We compensate for what we feel we lack in myriad ways—some good and some destructive. We "collect" change and start to believe it is who we are. But is it?

Perhaps the core of who we are does not change. Perhaps

we *are* like the land and at our core stay constant and serene and steady amidst all that we change on the surface. Some refer to this core as our authentic self. I just know that if I close my eyes and I don't think about the house I live in, the car I want, the people who hurt me, the critical view of myself in the mirror, the degree I have or don't have, the job, the kids, the spouse—all surface—I feel the same way I have always felt inside, at the core of who I am.

I will not stop changing my surface. I will still fuss and stew and muse and triumph and shift and reinvent. It's sort of my lifelong adventure: how many transformations can I make as a human being in this lifetime? And yet I am as grounded within as the land. We all are.

CHERRY GARCIA ICE CREAM

The rustle of the wind in the trees sounds the same wherever you are. Raindrops on a tin roof beat the same rhythm, cold air on a darkening night teases your skin, thunder in the distance quickens your heart, and sunlight through a dusty window warms the soul in the same familiar way. Nature is always at home.

I am sitting in a hotel in Vermont eating Cherry Garcia ice cream from a little cup with the tiniest spoon you can imagine, listening to music from the 1970s on my computer. I ate a prepackaged salad from the local grocery store for my dinner. It has been a long day and I am tired and very far from home. Yet my feet are tapping and I am happy.

A few weeks ago, I accepted a full-time Senior HR Director position, which takes me to distant cities for business. I was hesitant about this decision, which I knew would throw me back into the corporate world, but in some respects it was a test. Could I retain my inner sunshine and find a way to "tap my feet" if I was back in this profession? If I spent the entire day talking to people, listening to people, experiencing the idiocy that is inherent in any organization, could I still feel happy at the end of the day? My writing is all about finding the magic in everyday life. Well, folks, this is everyday life and you know what? Tonight, all alone in this hotel room, I still can find magic.

It is really quite simple. People matter. That's what my calling in life is, to help people. Many corporations do not recognize that they would not exist without the people. They view us as expenses. There wouldn't be a company without the people who are the company. And yet many times that simple fact does not seem to be valued. My calling compels me to bring that value to the workplace, both personally and professionally.

Most of us are just trying to make it in life. Trouble is, we find very unique ways of doing so. But beneath the sophisticated veneer of our fellow people, we all have common needs. Every day I talk to people who have a great desire to succeed, and who want to be recognized, valued, and appreciated. And if I smile, and I listen, I can feel the warmth in the room increase. This is not unique to me— it happens any time we allow our inner kindness to show. On some level people can connect in almost any situation, thanks to the power of positive energy and sharing who we are with others.

If you smile at someone tomorrow, see if you can feel the warmth in the room rise. And, even if it doesn't, tap your toes and eat ice cream when you get home! That is the magic of everyday life.

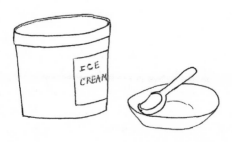

NEEDLE BLANKETS

The sun was shining brightly this morning but the air was chilled against my cheeks and the sky was filled with a colder clarity than I had grown accustomed to. Only a few weeks ago I had experienced a warm sunrise and a hazy summer sky. With the shift of seasons, I noticed how the sequoia and pine trees along my route seemed to be filled with brown needles overnight. These brown needles fell in heaps around the tree trunks as though a protective blanket for the changes soon to come. The old needles had fallen to pursue a new purpose while allowing the trees to prepare for new growth ahead.

We recently converted our old 8 mm movie films to the new technology of DVDs. These films include movies of my childhood. I watched these memories in fascination and thought about them for many days afterwards. As I walked this morning and noticed the blanket of old needles at the base of the tree trunks, I began to think about how we hold on to our past sometimes and we do not allow it to take its place and have its purpose in our own forward growth. The foundations of my childhood are certainly an intricate part of who I am today, but they should not inhibit who I become tomorrow. It is important to honor the past. The past provides us with lessons we can apply in the future. I do not believe the past should be a sacrificial monument for every belief and dream we have had or a mandate for how we should shape the rest of our life. Can we remember the past, examine it, and decide if it represents who we are today?

Studies have shown that the first six years of a child's life experience significantly impact who they are. I so believe this to be true, but I wonder if the first six years are defined by how others influence us and thereafter our life is defined by how we influence ourselves. Do we have the capacity to own our own life? Can we allow our past to nestle in our beginnings with love and respect, and to thrive with these experiences in their rightful place? I think it can be done, but it might be easier if we were a tree!

GRAY HAIR

Fog was lying softly in the low valleys, and the hilltops peeking above were strewn with the rich colors of the turning fall foliage. Though the sky was clear as the mighty sun emerged above the mountain, there was a chill that caught the earth by surprise—a subtle message that fall was the new CEO!

I was sitting across from my mother in a restaurant the other day and I could see her watching people. Suddenly from out of the blue she says, "I really don't like gray hair on people. I don't know why, but I just don't." As I looked at her with her permed gray hair I was speechless for a split second and then I just laughed. This was similar to the day she announced, "I hate green beans. I have always hated green beans and I'm never eating them again." This came from the mouth of a woman who was married to a man who grew acres of green beans, a woman who froze those acres of green beans and made those acres of green beans for dinner. I had no idea she did not like green beans. I found this candid honesty refreshing. It is not so different from the forthright opinions that come from the mouths of children. Often we laugh at the children, but we cringe at the frank statements from the elderly. But why should we not respond the same? The two groups are, after all, exactly where the circle of life meets. The rest of us are spread out over the continuum.

Children and the elderly exemplify the popular statement, "It is what it is."

That my mother did not find gray hair attractive stuck with me because she was making an observation about others that applied to her. How often do we do the same? How often is someone speechless when we make a judgment about someone else that reflects us, or them? We have based our relationships, our communication, our humor, our value systems on judgment. It is as if we would have nothing to say and no one to say it to if we stopped judging and instead considered what the truth might be for someone else.

I am a Deepak Chopra fan and in *The Seven Spiritual Laws of Success* he proposes that we should practice non-judgment, if even for a few moments. It is so easy to slip into this negative habit and it takes some work to stop ourselves in our tracks when we start down that path. If we work hard to remove judgment from our language and thought patterns, we can make a positive difference in our own world and the world around us.

We are all just people trying to do our best to find joy in the world. There is great wisdom in the proverb, "There, but for the grace of God, go I." Let your thoughts shift so that they might be more joyful and less judgmental today.

DIVINE QUILT

The smell of autumn wisps through the air and settles on the earth like the tapestry of a divine quilt. I visited a very special place on my walk today. Nestled among the tall firs is a rock inscribed with the word *Peace* and a handmade bench where one is able to sit and simply be. This place was created in honor of those who came before us left before us, and brought so much to our lives. It is a place that speaks to the circle of life. There is great stillness here today. The maple leaves have turned a golden yellow and they drift down upon this place and settle quietly as they prepare to return to the earth from whence they came. The fog is hanging heavily upon the hilltop. I feel the dampness of the air upon my face. Or, is it a caress from a love I can no longer touch?

While often I focus on positivity and possibility, I wish to recognize that there are losses in life that bring us to our knees. Sometimes these losses happen as a result of physical illness and death. Sometimes the losses happen slowly with aging, addictions, or other life circumstances. I do not believe that we learn humility without being humbled, or that we learn compassion without times of difficulty and suffering. These are the times when we are most challenged, and often when we are most touched, in heart and soul. Regardless of how balanced we may think we are, or whether we have come to terms with our loss over time, there are occasions when, quite unexpectedly, years might as well be minutes and we are engulfed by the pain as though it were yesterday.

I have experienced significant losses in my life. I am not unique in this. All people have experienced deeply defining moments, and if you could see into their world, you would find this to be true, even though their appearance would never have you believe this. I will not for a second pretend that I walk through life without the sharp edge of loss stopping me in my tracks when I least expect it, but even in those moments of remembering, I understand that I feel the darkness because of the light of love. If love did not exist in the first place, I would not feel the pain. And I am grateful that it is the love that prevails in my memories and my life. I celebrate the absolute joy of being capable of loving, and remembering the loving, so that it shapes my life every day in a positive way. I feel honored to have experienced relationships and love this deeply and I will gladly accept the anguish rather than lose the love.

Today, remember that everyone, regardless of who they are or what position they hold, hides within them a significant loss. Honor it in yourself and honor it in others. Let compassion guide you and may love always prevail.

FOGGY LACE

The fog was hanging thick against the trees and grasses like a cloak of fine mist, turning the spider webs to exquisite lace orbs along the fences. This is a rare and special day. Only these conditions create the magic of the webs and many times it happens only one day a year. Some years it does not happen at all. Suddenly, all those invisible webs are brought into full, intricate view. Even the low-lying cobwebs in the grass transform into gossamer blankets. As soon as the sun breaks through, the lace is gone and the webs slip back into invisibility.

Spider-web days offer a view of the spectacular in a most unexpected way. You must pay attention to the magic in everyday life or you will miss these days entirely. Paying attention is one of the most important aspects of finding magic in odd places. I have learned more by simply paying attention than I have in any other way. Observation and curiosity feed our minds and free us from the mundane. Without these qualities, inventions and discoveries of all kinds would never occur. I love to see the passion for learning and living and experiencing life in the people around me. This passion is why I am so in love with children. They see what we don't see because their minds are not cluttered and their curiosity is alive every moment.

Sometimes we must make a concentrated effort to drag our adult minds out from the barrage of information and activity around us and just pay attention. I watch our world swirl with technology and multitasking and wonder if we will suffer from all of this. Do we ever give our attention to any one thing? Do we sit in meetings and actually listen? Or are we sending messages on our cell phones and laptops while planning our next strategy? What do we miss by not paying attention? What could we learn and see and know simply by being curious again? How much more successful would we be if we spent more time paying attention?

Spider webs on a foggy day. Mundane turned magic. Reminders that if we pay attention, what was invisible becomes crystal clear. And even if the webs fade back into the sunlight, our world will have expanded.

LIPSTICK

The path was strewn with golden leaves that had fallen in the briskness of a night wind. Occasionally a lone leaf drifted down in a sweeping dance, defining elegance and grace. All around me the world was spun with gold more stunning than words could ever describe. A stillness I could feel, a breath that exposed changes to come.

As I drove off to an errand today, our elderly neighbor lady was picking her way along the gravel road as she returned from the mailbox. Over the last year, she has grown frail, thin, and unsteady on her feet. She takes small, hesitant steps. Her rather wild gray hair was sticking out from under the cap she wore and she barely raised her hand in greeting as I passed. But, I noticed with great amusement, she had on her carefully applied bright red lipstick! My elderly, equally frail, mother never leaves the house without making sure her lipstick is on. This ritual is almost like a beacon of life: *I am alive, I will survive, because I've got my lipstick. I might not be able to walk, I might not be able to talk, I might even need extra oxygen to breathe, but I've got my lipstick!* Love it!

Watching our neighbor slowly, painfully, make the trek on the gravel road always causes me to consider turning around and taking her the rest of the way home. And on rainy days I do. But on pretty days like today, I resist this compulsion of mine. As much as I want to help, I also understand that this daily path she walks ever so carefully is giving her a sense of pride and purpose. No longer able to drive, at least the walk gives her a taste of independence. It would not be a good thing to take this from her. Aging deprives us of independence. My mother is always saying, "I don't do anything for anyone." She craves a sense of purpose even though her limitations provide few opportunities to carry that out.

Watching my mother age is a place where I exercise the flow of life, but only because I don't have any choice in the matter. I honestly don't know what to do. I have to trust life and pray for compassion, patience, and grace. The only guide I have is love. No matter what I do, it isn't going to be better. Little Miss Fix It can't fix this. I can learn from it, however. I can expand who I am from living this with my mother even though there are many days when the expansion feels a lot more like pain.

Being with my mom is the quickest method of slowing my pace. I must step back to meet the needs of my mother. I see this in our world, this rapid-fire way we live and how the older people in our life lose the ability to race along with us. Meaningful conversations happen with fewer words and longer pauses but those conversations are more appreciated by my mom than by anyone else I can think of.

If we believe that kindness matters to all, then we need to multiply the impact by a million when we apply this to the elderly. One kind word, one smile—whether we know the person or not—will carry joy that we cannot imagine. And if we are lucky, they will be inspired to put on more lipstick!

TWIRL

The October rain was pelting the windows this morning. The falling leaves were driven on their journey by the force of an autumn wind. This was not a day for drifting and dancing leaves in a lazy choreography of color. They were speeding to their destination with no time for twirling.

We seem to be like the leaves as we move toward our own destinations. There are times when we speed rapidly to our goals, driven by the forces of life straight to where we need to be. Then there are other times when we take an uncertain, twirling path—dancing, floating, mesmerized by the wind and sidetracked by the movements of the dance. The dancing journey is more fun and peaceful, but we are not a twirling, flowing species. We seem to believe that unless we are driving straight towards our planned and plotted destination, we are failing to be a productive and responsible person. Interestingly enough, unless life intends for us to move quickly and precisely, we still end up dipping and swirling and drifting away from the very goal we believe we must reach. We need to learn that twirling is okay—that we don't always have to know exactly where we are going and that sometimes we end up in very special places if we let the winds of life take us there.

Allow the flow of life to unfold. The more I try to

control my life and drive it forward, the more restrictions I experience, the less I accomplish, and the worse I feel. I often have to make a conscious effort to step back and allow life to lead—feel the dance—and amazingly enough the direction I have been trying to contrive simply happens before me with the grace and ease of the twirling leaves. Stepping back means releasing the fears that drive us forward in a gallant but unsuccessful attempt to make life happen. We must learn to let life happen and continue to trust the dance.

Today I am going to watch the leaves twirl and let life twirl as well. Tomorrow may find me racing toward my goals with the wind behind me. But today, I'm going to twirl.

GLEE

The leaves were crowded upon the ground, having fallen from the trees in an autumn wind. I began my day by running through the piles of leaves with two laughing little boys while waiting for the school bus. Their glee at the crunching and swishing beneath our feet was heart stopping. This is called play. As adults, we don't do enough of that. Glee seems to vanish from our productive, responsible lives.

One of the reasons I so enjoy spending an entire day with my grandsons is I can play. My entire center of attention is on being with my grandchildren. We play games for the sake of games and not for the sake of winning, we eat shaped sandwiches, play hide-and-seek for enjoyment rather than survival, we make up stories without endings for the sheer pleasure of the telling, we color and draw for no grade or approval, we swing and dance with abandon, and fall asleep with smiles on our faces. These little people delight and amuse me and are my therapy in a fast-paced, goal-driven world. For just this day, this time, I don't have any goal but to love them and enjoy my time in their presence. I am renewed, though exhausted.

As we grow older, we find exhaustion comes more easily. I wonder if it is because we are so consumed by being an adult that we no longer know how to play. The physical activity we experience with children is daunting in itself but the real exhaustion comes from the mental stimulation we experience when we are with children. One must be on their toes! Children force us to use that creative, imaginative side of our brain to go back to a time when rolling on the floor, *ribbit*-ing like a frog, chasing balls, and playing make-believe came naturally. Perhaps this inactivity of the spontaneous side of ourselves is why adults so dislike role-play exercises in management training. We are out of practice and out of our comfort zone. We are too concerned about whether or not we will do it "right."

I think that I should receive continuing education credits for the days I spend with my grandchildren. I learn more from them about thinking outside of the box than from any management or leadership training class I will ever attend. I learn win/win negotiation skills, multitasking and prioritizing strategies (crying and bleeding move to the top) . . . and I love learning it!

My wish for you today is that you find some way to play and rekindle your love of learning.

GOLDEN THREADS

A flurry of tiny leaves caught in my hair as I passed beneath the glory of the trees. All around me the vibrant golden leaves echoed a stark contrast to the tall evergreens on the hilltop. There was a crunch beneath my feet on dry leaves already fallen to the earth to begin a new journey. The shifts and changes of autumn were all around me.

Our lives are constantly shifting and changing. It is the way of things. We sometimes lament, however, that the relationships that were so important, so much a part of our life, shift and change as life moves around us. Job changes, relocations, children growing up, aging, activities coming and goingthese all create human relationship shifts. Our focus moves away from what was to what is and very few people are with us throughout the journey.

In thinking with sadness about the loss of significant relationships, I realized that this movement is really a lesson about living in the present, bringing love to the moment. As mortals, we do not have the capacity to retain and nurture each relationship that we encounter. Instead, we learn from each and move forward to the next lesson. Though our focus is suddenly different, and the people in our lives suddenly replaced, what we leave behind is the golden thread. How we live in each moment becomes our tapestry, our fabric, our living quilt.

Each relationship is a thread in more hues than we can possibly imagine, connected to an infinite spool that never leaves our souls. The threads of each relationship are interwoven to create who we become. How we live, and love, in each moment of our life and in each relationship we have becomes part of us and what we give to the world. It is important, then, to bring the best of ourselves to every moment, for what we give and do in each moment will remain with us on the entire journey of life.

As my daughter grew up, a wonderful poster hung on her wall that read: "What you are is God's gift to you. What you become is your gift to God." We come into this world with our own special gifts—each one of us. What we do with those gifts, in each moment we live, becomes our own unique and exquisite expression of gratitude.

May you give generously in each moment so the hue of your thread leaves a gracious stitch in the tapestry of others.

SPLENDOR WITHIN

From every window in my home, yellow leaves greet me. As I walk along the driveway, a canopy of the same glory surrounds me. Wherever I travel, the splendor of the autumn leaves is evident. These beautiful displays nature has provided for us are simply astounding and captivate me beyond words.

The leaves on the trees are visual reminders of the magic of nature and the universe. They are tangible expressions of wonder and power. And yet the true magic lies within the limbs and trunks where we are unable to see the depth, the motion, the movement that creates what we see in the present moment. Beneath the surface, beneath the colors that awe us each day, is the work of free-flowing energy.

Humans are much the same. We live in glory in mere moments. We triumph and twirl and bow in small segments of life. Yet the work, the magic, of arriving to that glory lies far beneath the surface deep within each of us as we struggle to understand what our souls are trying to teach us. All the thoughts and lessons and challenges we face each day lead us to the brilliance of an autumn day in the sun. It is important for us to comprehend that the outer show is simply a show and what is truly important is what we cannot see within. This inner glory guides us, and when the leaves have fallen from our tree, it remains.

Perhaps the splendor of the leaves is a reminder to honor the greater splendor of the magnificence within each of us. How we live within ourselves determines the brilliance of our leaves.

RAIN WALK

The pouring rain battered the fragile clinging leaves on the autumn trees, creating a watery carpet of those already fallen to the earth below. I walked in the rain. There was no umbrella to protect me but I wanted it this way. I wanted to feel the water, hoping it would bring clarity to my thoughts this day. Though my head was bent, I yearned to see beyond my own footsteps. If you want to see more, you must lift your face. Even in the rain. So I did.

My thoughts were centered on ego—a three-letter word considered a four-letter word in our lessons about good and evil. I wondered if we were giving ego a bad rap. I pondered how it was different from pride, perceived for the most part as the Good Witch. The greatest spiritual people have somehow learned how to give up ego and pride and all the other characteristics that create havoc for humans. However, most of us may never reach that level of living. So, what do we do with qualities like ego?

After much contemplation, I came to the conclusion that the real issue with ego and pride is that they are fragile. They can be shattered so easily. Consider how our days can plummet in an instant after receiving criticism from others— we'll review even the smallest comment over and over— because our ego has been wounded. We have received input that immediately sends us into self-doubt and the world of "lesser than" and "imperfection." We spend precious moments trying desperately to justify, to modify, to mollify our sense of self—our pride, our ego. Even when ego seems to be rather garish and bold, it really is very weak, and the only power it has is defining us in ways that we should not allow it to.

Yet we are humans with this bountiful world of emotion that makes us so compelling and unique. I can ponder this all I want, but I still must live with my ego and my pride. The key seems to be taking a step back and being just a little reflective about it sometimes. Walk in the rain without an umbrella and let the reality of the raindrops on your face be a guide for the times when you need to wash away what really doesn't matter. Ego and pride are what we allow them to be. They lower our heads and limit our sight. Lift your face to the rain.

GIN AND JEANS

The tree stood tall, dark, and strong, its branches spanning across the yard, flung wide to touch the deepening gray of the clouds beyond. In contrast, lacy leaves of golden yellow and orange clung delicately to the limbs, some slipping from their grasp and cascading to the earth to dance with the tossing wind—a waltz of autumn splendor.

On occasion, I succumb to the ills of the common cold. So it was yesterday. When I was young, my mother would make me sweet, hot lemonade to soothe my symptoms. So, I decided that I should try this remedy with a slight modification. I had my husband make me a lemon drop martini. After the first one, I felt a little better but not yet as well as I remember feeling when I was young after the lemon beverage from Mom. So, I had my husband make another. Mmmmm . . . *Now* it was starting to work like I remembered!

A few years ago, I was having one of those days when I just felt frumpy. I had seen martini bars all over the place and I figured martinis must be something pretty special if they had entire establishments dedicated to them. So, off we went to a martini bar. It was quite posh and filled with savvy people sipping away. I took my first drink and thought I had just consumed a mouthful of rubbing alcohol. No, I did not spit it across the table or gag. I'm quite sure my eyes got very big and my husband had a hard time controlling his mirth. (He could have warned me.) The last time this smell had lingered in my stinging nostrils was when I had to pump gas by hand into the tractor. However, I was determined to "unfrump" myself and not let anyone know that I was really a country bumpkin, so I sipped this drink for an hour pretending I was having just as grand a time as all those other pretending people. Since then, I have acquired (and it truly takes acquiring) enough taste that I can handle lemon drop martinis—if you put enough sugar around the edge!

I have this vision for a marketing ad: Picture a martini bar in the jeans section of the department store. The store would have soft lights and you could only enter if you had stopped and sipped at least two martinis. The agony of purchasing jeans—who in the world came up with a size zero! —would be greatly diminished, and sales would skyrocket. They have it all wrong in stores today with their fluorescent lights and mirrors two feet away—you don't even have the slimming effect of distance. Those jeans that look so huge they couldn't possibly be your size send you straight to depression when you put them on and they won't even fit over your hips. The experience brings a whole new definition to low riders! Imagine how much more fun it would be if your vision were skewed by a martini or two.

I know that we should all find self-acceptance. I read all those books, too. Reading them, however, doesn't make it easier when you have a frumpy day. (Or try on new jeans.) To regain my perspective on those days, I think of the people who have impacted my life the most; it is not their body size I remember, but the size of their heart.

ALPENGLOW

A phenomenon called alpenglow occurs at sunset, when a glow is found on the mountains and the clouds in the opposite direction from where you would expect to find the light of a gathering sunset. Nature's brushstroke turns the mountains and clouds to a subtle, almost iridescent pink that graces the landscape with a soft light. The sunrise is bolder and peeks from the back of the mountains and clouds; this is what we have come to expect each day. It is glorious and awe inspiring, but very different from the view of alpenglow. Alpenglow seems to come from the angels as they drift off to sleep.

My very special friend—the one I laughed with, cried with, knew from all angles—suffered a brain aneurysm and then a stroke a few years ago, which left her significantly impaired both physically and cognitively. I have struggled to accept this monumental loss with varying degrees of success. When I go to visit my friend, our visits are sometimes blessed with short minutes of insightful conversation and sometimes there is virtually no conversation at all. I have learned to go with no expectations and feel humbled when the moments of connection are present. When they are not, I have learned to simply communicate with her in silence, on a different level. However, many times when I visit her, she says very clearly,

"Hi, Heidi" and will tell me, "You are so beautiful." There are days when those are the *only* words she speaks.

Now, I am confident about many things in my life but appearance has never been one of them. My perspective is shaped by magazines, books, movies, photos, and other media. Appearance is my greatest area of insecurity, and I believe this applies to many others as well. However, my friend's definition of beauty is one to ponder and learn from on many levels—not just for how I see myself, but for how I perceive others. She may tell others who visit her that they are beautiful, and that makes it even more profound, for she is communicating from a distant place a message of great importance to this world. Like the alpenglow, she reflects to us a beauty that is different from what we expect to see, a beauty far more astounding than our limited vision allows us to understand. I have not achieved this understanding yet but that subtle message she has delivered makes me *want* to understand and makes me question myself when I make judgments based on definitions that are shaped by external measures.

Some of the greatest lessons we learn are from the most painful of circumstances. Though I have shed many tears over my friend's limitations, I know that I have been blessed by talking with this angel who has not yet been released to fly. I hope I am listening well.

Do not take for granted the people you love. Believe in the inconceivable. Listen to the angels in your life even if you cannot see their wings.

BEAUTY AND THE BEAST

The cornstalks were rustling in the wind—whispering—with their browning dresses and frills. It was an October chatter as though they were excited in anticipation of harvest moons, frosty pumpkins, and swirling leaves. The smell of wood smoke from a distant fire was skipping across the breeze. Nature was calling the summer world to return to the soft, familiar space of earth below. Homecoming.

There are two times a year when blackberry vines show off their own version of splendor: when they produce delicate pink blossoms in early summer and when their leaves turn a rich yellow in the fall. The rest of the year, even when the berries are sweet and ripe, the foliage is really quite obnoxious with their prickly vines and invasion of the land.! How deceiving beauty can be.

People are not much different sometimes from the blackberries. There are those who are dazzlingly beautiful and suave. We are in awe of their appearance and judge them to be exquisite all the way through. Quite surprised are we when we feel the sharp sting beneath the beauty and become tangled in thorny vines that wish to control us. On the contrary, there are also those who flaunt their annoying traits openly. We cower and judge them to be crusty and cruel from outside to inside. We are surprised, then, when we catch a glimpse of insecurity and kindness slip from beneath the barbs and bravado. It doesn't, perhaps, make them people we want to know, but it does give us a much different perspective, and tolerance for their hostile and inappropriate behaviors.

Let's face it. We are judgment junkies and we really aren't all that adept at it. As a species, we have been granted the gift and curse of critical thinking. Unfortunately, many times it is just that—critical—and our judgments are uninformed and based on our own experiences and assumptions. In many aspects of our world, we are capable in our ability to judge. When it comes to our relationships with people, our abilities are limited.

It is hard not to judge, but judgment inflicts wounds that are often never forgotten. I believe each of us has felt that kind of judgment at some time in our lives. And I believe each of us has been surprised to find thorns where we didn't expect them, and beauty buried in places we discovered by accident. We should always entertain the fact that we "don't know what we don't know." If we can step back from our judgments and recognize we are making them based on limited information, maybe we will be more cautious in showing our thorns to others.

My father worked on the railroad. He often told me how he held the railroad "bums" in high esteem because when they got off the train, they always gave their dog a drink before taking one themselves. While my father did not live his life the way these folks did, he did not judge them with disdain. He recognized the kindness and saw the good. May I do the same.

TEETERING

The trees were not dancing in the wind today—they were whipping and lashing about. I glanced at my tall tree friends and felt a moment of fear for their well-being, hoping their roots were deep and strong as the tumultuous weather tossed them about. With my hood pulled up, hands in my pockets, I made my way and found the wind refreshing and fierce.

At times I find life this way. When we make the decision to set off on a journey that will push us into something new, we feel fear and exhilaration at the same time. So much is unknown to us, and we are eager to learn. There are times, however, when the journey is not one we have deliberately chosen. Those times, we feel the fierceness rather than the thrill of a new adventure. We become vulnerable and our courage teeters dangerously before us.

This time of year, we often experience nesting syndrome. We prepare for the cold days and long nights ahead with extra food in the cupboard, firewood on the porch, batteries in the flashlights, warm coats and new socks. We are ready. And we know with absolute certainty that the harshness of winter will end and turn to spring.

When life hands us a winter experience—cold, dark, fierce—or an adventure we did not anticipate, we struggle to regain our balance. We are caught unaware and feel we do not have the spiritual provisions we need. We do not feel the certainty that spring will be waiting for us at the end of the darkness. So we are afraid.

We all experience fear. I work consciously to let the fear go but I am not always successful. My faith that we have far more spiritual provisions than we know and that life unfolds for a reason regardless of how it looks in the moment keeps me from running for shelter from the darkness. As George Harrison so eloquently sang in "Beware of Darkness," darkness and sadness are "not what you are here for." Still, I recognize that the amount of strength it takes to overcome these can be immense. It takes courage to find the joy when life seems fierce.

May you know with absolute certainty deep within that you are prepared for the spiritual journeys of your life. May fear fade to the shadows on your path and may love be your guiding light.

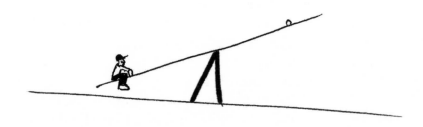

SIMPLICITY

It is the first day of November, my very favorite month of the year. I love the days when the rain batters the windows, the leaves fly through the air in twirling flurries, the animals contentedly curl up by the fire, and so do the humans. Thanksgiving sometimes feels like it is the forgotten holiday, but I love it. Perhaps because it is not so hectic as the Christmas rush. Perhaps because it promotes a time to be thankful for all that we have been given that we often take for granted. Perhaps because it is the one time of year you can get away with telling someone to "get stuffed"!

Certain tasks I simply do not like to do. There are no commonsense reasons that apply to my disenchantment but I am very consistent in my resistance. One task is emptying the silverware from the dishwasher. I have been known to wash the silverware three times before I finally break down and put it away in the drawer. This generally follows a frustrating search for a spoon or fork that is tangled amidst the measuring spoons in the dishwasher. (My father always said we should just have three dishwashers and forget the cupboards. Maybe he had a point after all.)

I also do not like to put my recipes back in their appropriate organizer. It wouldn't be that difficult or take that much time, but I have a tendency to toss them in a pile in the cupboard. They accumulate in this chaotic state and I continue to grumble as I leaf through the pile time and again to find what I'm looking for. Eventually I sit down and file them all back in their very pathetic packets, folders, and boxes and vow to be more diligent in my organizational skills. (It is actually amazing that they still stay in those packets, folders, and boxes because after thirty years these "tools" are ripped, taped, spilled upon, and stuffed until they are barely functional.)

My other task that screams procrastination is folding socks. My preference would be to dump them in a pile in the window seat and let my husband fend for himself. The problem is, the cats find them a very nice spot to rest and my husband is rather colorblind. These are not conducive to the "Tidy Heidi syndrome! Furry or mismatched socks are like a billboard announcing my failure as a woman.

The motions of routine life—our comfort zones and the imperfections that follow us as we strive to be perfect—are fascinating. The places we scurry to when life doesn't work out like we hoped. The peace we find in simple pleasures and moments. I love it when the sun slants off a clean kitchen floor (a rare occasion); when I can sit at one end of the house and look to the other end and everything is clean, warm, and in its place; Sunday night dinners on new placemats; lunch with candles; kittens curled in a chair; new pictures of our grandchildren on the desk; lamplight on beloved books; steam from a coffee cup rising in the morning air; the feel of new socks on my feet; the sound of the furnace running on a cold day; the smell of grass; a new bird on an old feeder. Everyday occurrences. Sublime snippets of life.

May you have more tasks you love than those you don't, may you appreciate the simple things that really do make up a life, and may peace be your companion in this beautiful season.

WINGS IN FLIGHT

The wind was warm for the first of November. The trees were bending from the wind, sending showers of golden leaves swirling across the land; cascades of twirling helicopter maple seeds filled the sky. All across the landscape, dots of orange and yellow mixed with the constancy of the green fir and pine trees to give this blustery day a beauty that was simply awesome. A finer day could not be found in all of autumn's offerings. It stirred absolute gratitude within me that I could share in the glory of this breathtaking beauty.

Some days we revel in the wind and some days we run from it. The wind is not something you can control. It will have its way regardless of what you wish for. The absolute power of nature. I was reminded of the force and flow of the wind as four jet fighters flew overhead the other day.

I have always loved to watch the jet fighters fly. As I stopped to watch them, a flock of birds sharing the same sky view caught my eye. This made for quite a comparison. The jets went zooming through the air with a focused, structured, rigid purpose. The birds could out maneuver the jets with ease. They swooped, adjusted, and chattered, accomplishing their purpose with agility and a grace the jets could not begin to match. The birds move with the wind and the jets push through it. People try to live like the jets—rigid, focused, noisy, and forceful against the natural currents of living. I want to live my life like the birds—flexible, graceful, moving like a dance, turning on a dime, moving with the life around me, letting it go, and accomplishing my purpose with ease and grace and delight.

I admire the purpose and accomplishments of people who overcome great odds by pushing at life. Yet if I could, I'd choose to live life with less force and more flow. I have thought a bit about this. First, could I do it? I'm a determined person. It's hard to just "flow" when there are so many things to do. Perhaps it is how you approach those things, how you think about what it is you have to do, and how many times you smile or laugh when you do them that create the dance instead of the flight plan. It will take some practice!

SEASONS OF LIFE

The neon lights of autumn are captivating. The trees are in their glory with more nuances of color than humans could create on their very best day. The leaves dance and glitter in the sunlight with an occasional solo performance as they spiral downward, pulled to the captivating beat of the earth.

It is surprising that I have not run into mailboxes, cars, or ditches lately. You see, I am so enthralled with the beautiful autumn leaves that I am continually gawking at them as I drive, awed by their brilliance and spectacular colors, even on rainy days. I love the days when they swirl down from the trees and dance on the streets below. I become distracted and have to force myself to pay attention to the road ahead.

This time of year makes me think about the changing seasons and the changing life of the trees. I have often heard these changes equated to human life as well. In the spring, the trees burst with new life, growing rapidly every day with a refreshing spirit of hope, as childhood is for mankind. In the summer, the trees rustle in the warm breezes, flowing and swaying easily as they provide a backdrop for energetic sunny days, as humans do as they grow and learn moving to adulthood. In the autumn, the trees turn glorious colors, announcing their presence with a flare that is awe inspiring, flaunting their gifts with brilliance – as humankind does in their maturing adulthood. In the winter, the trees are barren and stark, bracing themselves against the whipping cold winds and downpours—as elderly humans do? Oh my! I'm in the middle of the fall leaves of life and I'm not liking where this analogy is going at all.

What is the one thing that can turn the stark and barren trees of winter into something as spectacular as the trees in the rest of the seasons? Christmas lights! So, when that season of life comes upon me, I will wrap myself up with twinkling lights, plug myself in, and radiate light and energy to dazzle the world. I feel much better now. I'm counting on unfaltering electricity.

It is my greatest hope that I can find the inner light in all seasons of my life so that I might shine throughout life regardless of outer appearances. May what we bring to life today serve as the unfaltering power for our tomorrows.

SOGGY SOCKS

On a wet and windy November day, my shoes made a squishing sound as I walked, and there was a constant hum in the trees as the rain fell upon them. Occasionally there was a gust of wind and the percussion of the rain intensified before returning to the steady rhythm. Across the valley I could see the rain sweeping in sync with the wind and I knew the golden leaves still clinging to the trees would be gone before week's end.

As I trudged along, I thought about how much this morning mimicked the soggiest spring day. The steady rain was the same, the temperature equivalent, and the wind was blowing from the same direction as the March winds. And yet this day felt colder and I felt older. I find it very intriguing how we view these same facts of weather differently in the fall than in the spring. In the fall we feel a quiet sense of resignation on a day like this. In the spring, we are elated because the day is bringing flowers and green to our landscape. Today is the beginning of nature's task of bringing us those delightful, hopeful things, although we see only the barren trees and darkening skies. How fascinating we are!

Perception and interpretation are very curious. These qualities truly are what make us all so interesting. I was a winter-born baby. I spent my first days buried under a warm blanket listening to the wind and the rain from a place of infant peace. Today I am perfectly content to do much the same. It is curious to me how much we are affected by where we are, when, and how we feel at the time. All along our path in life, we have different experiences and they form our attitudes and thoughts about all kinds of things. If we lived in a totally rigid mindset, how boring we would be.

The facts of any situation might be absolute, but our view of these facts is absolutely our own. Our opinions can be limiting since we incorporate our own experiences into our perceptions unless we try to at least catch a glimpse of how the situation could be perceived differently by someone else. Most importantly, this awareness of the views of others can change our own perception. Then we expand our world.

May I remember to step back and acknowledge that I am seeing life through my window of experiences and recognize and appreciate the windows of others who are not seeing it exactly the same. May I allow my experiences and my perceptions to enhance and broaden the view from my window rather than limit what I can see.

THANKS GIVING

The leaves have slipped from the trees and barren branches are etched against the palest of pink clouds in the November sunrise. Remnants of golden glory are shifting to brown blankets on the earth, and on dry, windy days they scurry off to unknown territories to rest for the winter and nurture the spring to come. Wood smoke curls around my nostrils, the twittering of winter birds hovers in the air, my breath drifts across the air like mist, and I scurry to the warmth of my home.

This is the season for gratitude. Thanksgiving is my favorite holiday, for it turns our thoughts to what we have rather than what we have not. I believe that many of us make a conscious effort to be grateful for what we have. Sometimes, though, we simply "think" it. We make a list in our minds of the things we are thankful for and run through it often, priding ourselves on how grateful we are and how often we express our thanks. But the power of gratitude is that it shifts us to a peaceful, content, and happy place. "Thinking" our gratitude doesn't take us there. We must "feel" our gratitude to find the joy in it.

I, too, fall prey to making that list in my mind. I really have to force myself to stop amidst my busyness and feel the gratitude. When I do this, I feel the total joy of being with my grandsons in their yellow raincoats, frog boots, and

Spider Man umbrellas, splashing in the puddles to see how wet they can possibly get. I feel the contentment of a blanket curled around my feet with a relaxed cat on my lap purring and smiling, his bliss becoming my bliss. I feel the peace and love of sitting in front of the fire with a glass of good red wine, sharing my day with a husband who is my friend and my love. I feel the distinct pleasure of crawling into bed between heavenly fleece sheets, listening to the rain outside my window.

Gratitude is not an exercise of the mind, but of the heart. Yes, do make that list. But then take the moments to feel the gratitude. If you do this, I promise that you will feel the joy move from your toes all the way to your nose.

GRATITUDE LOG

The wind swept through the trees in a flourishing dance of excitement and survival. The last leaves on their swirling branches plummeted to the ground below. Only the driving rain kept the golden moss of already fallen leaves from being hurled to foreign places amongst the forest and the fields. The weather was the epitome of Winnie the Pooh's blustery day.

For several years, my family has participated in the tradition of a Yule log. The Yule log, burned on Christmas, allegedly brings you good fortune for the year to come. Perhaps we are not thinking the right thoughts, but we have not found a significant correlation between the Yule log and the success of our year.

This year we designed a Gratitude Log, instead, to be burned on Thanksgiving. The little ones gather pinecones to toss into the fire after we place the Gratitude Log there; with each pinecone they say something they are grateful for. (Little boys love to toss pinecones in the fire, so we can always expect a very long gratitude list.) The Gratitude Log is not about what we anticipate for the future, but what we are thankful for in the present. There will be many opportunities to look forward to new and exciting things, but on this day of Thanksgiving, we will be thinking of all we already have.

There is a great scene in the movie *While You Were*

Sleeping when a young lady without any family inadvertently finds herself seated at the holiday table of an exuberant and rather dysfunctional family. As she observes the disjointed conversations and personalities around that table, she is warmed by the fact that she is sharing the holiday meal rather than being by herself. Sometimes when families gather together, there is a tendency to focus on the turkeys around the table rather than the ones *on* the table, and we have visions of stuffing something, or someone, other than the bird. This year, if we appreciate our surroundings like the young lady in the movie, we, too, will find the privilege of sharing our holiday with family and friends—in spite of their dysfunction. (And ours.)

May happiness settle upon you on this day of thanks and giving.

CLOUDY SUNRISE

The horizon began warming with a soft pink washed across the clouds. In a matter of moments, the softness turned to rich, vibrant coral, encompassing the eastern sky, each cloud a brilliant burst of beauty from the brush of the sun. Magnificence!

From the window of an early morning airplane, I once watched the sun rise, high above the dense blanket of clouds hanging over the earth below. A ribbon of brilliant light skimmed the horizon before the sun washed the sky to an even blue. While spectacular, it did not have the artistic depth of the clouds awash with shades and hues and shapes that were part of the sunrise I had seen today.

For a while, clouds had been with me and I was unable to touch the peace and joy I find most days. I had been so focused on the "clouds" that I was unable to view the peaceful, beautiful elements of life. The sunrise today made me think. Without the clouds—whether in the sunrise or in life—the magnificence would diminish. Clouds capture our inner light and reflect it back to others with a richness and a depth that could not be experienced without them. Certainly there is beauty in a cloudless sunrise, and a cloudless life, but the splendor is less stunning, less impactful.

In my most philosophical moments, I recognize

the need for the challenges that clouds bring to our days. Without the comparison, without knowing how to rebalance ourselves when things are not perfect, I suppose life would be pretty boring. It is the days when all my philosophy is in a muddled heap that I have trouble remembering the benefit of clouds. The sunrise today was a welcome message that we must always keep in our minds and our hearts—that behind those clouds there is always light. We capture it, it becomes us, and we are magnificent.

PURRING

Clouds were skipping through the surrounding hilltops on the heels of a brisk southwest wind that played with the air like swirling ribbons. Clinging to the very tips of the pine needles were perfect iridescent spheres of rain that had fallen in the night. Only on special days with just the right conditions do the drops of rain linger on the needles this way. It is a phenomenon that fills me with gratitude that I am able to experience these things I love.

I also love that cats purr. It is such an honest, forthright expression of happiness. Uncontrolled, spontaneous, and totally sincere, a fascinating trait that humans do not have. I wish, though, that humans purred. How nice it would be to know if true happiness, in the moment, was emanating from a fellow human. Humans are so good at pretending. Cats are good at pretending, too, but not about happiness.

Dogs also project their happiness in a spontaneous, honest way. They wag their tails and the happier they are, the faster it wags. I love the popular bumper sticker that states, "Wag more, bite less." What a terrific reminder for us to find a space and place of happiness more often and to avoid the churning, impatient side of living.

I thought about this wagging and purring for a while. What do humans possess that is even close to these unique expressions? Laughing. Yes, I think laughing is how we purr and wag. When we laugh, we truly express our mirth and the happiness flows through our veins for hours. Yet our society has rules about laughing; there are no purring and wagging rules. I know I have been in meetings where I found the "serious" topics quite amusing, and to laugh at that time would have been inappropriate and had some not too pleasant consequences. I admit, internally I was rolling in the aisle, and even that held my happiness flow for quite some time.

I comply with the laughing rules but I do think we should laugh more often—freely and with joy. If we find the amusement in ourselves and the world around us, life is easier. Serious issues require serious consideration, but taking *ourselves* too seriously diminishes our ability to share the best of who we are with others. We are truly delightful creatures who simply forget the power of purring.

LINGERING

The air is very still today. Leaves make their journey back to earth in single file, gently sliding from the tree in a solitary path. If you step outside, you can smell the rain, although it has not yet arrived. From my windows I see only masses of golden leaves still clinging to the trees. They are so beautiful.

I made time today for an extra cup of coffee and took a few minutes to simply gaze at the loveliness of the scene before me, trying somehow to imprint this splendor in my mind so that I might remember it long after this day. All too soon my view will be of dark and barren branches against a stark sky. I want to linger.

Linger. I like that word. It suggests quieter moments, suspended sweetness, and inner peace. It is warm and rich and rebellious against the fast pace of life. It is living in a moment that pleases us just a little longer. A lingering moment is a moment of gratitude—a time when our soul sighs with pleasure and appreciates the wonder of life. It is a feeling that is rich and full and almost tangible. It is a gift we give to ourselves on rare occasions, and it is heavenly. Lingering lasts only a matter of moments, but renews our spirit for hours.

I can go for days and never find a lingering moment. When one arrives, I remember how wonderful this experience is, for I am living the gratitude, living the beauty of the moment, and my heart is happy. It is how you feel as you drift off to sleep or wake from a sweet dream. It fills all the busy spaces with a sense of well-being and serenity.

I promise myself to hold on to lingering moments like the one I found today, and to simply absorb the beauty in life.

KALEIDOSCOPE

The mornings are dark now. I can no longer watch the dawn slip into the sky as I begin my days. I am well into the "must dos" of the morning routine before the light lifts the veil of hidden land. I miss waking up to the cheerful countenance of the sun.

I am a person of passion and purpose. I work for companies with people-driven missions and bring deep convictions with me wherever I go. I was born this way it seems. I find this passion propels me into a life filled to the brim no matter what circumstances surround me. The kaleidoscope of my life shifts constantly, revealing soft images at times and sharp, poignant ones at others. I must continually step back from my tendency to force the hand of life and instead let it flow freely, allowing the shifts and the changes and recognizing the beauty of each moment. I am continually challenged by my own expectations of my ability to live life in a more perfect way. I know I am not unique in this.

I think much of what we do is counterproductive to how we want to feel. We often spend much time and thought ensuring that others are okay, and yet we do not exude the same devotion to making sure that *we* are okay. We are generous in our acceptance and forgiveness of others and expend great energy chastising ourselves. We do not approach others with the expectation that they will be perfect and yet we have that very expectation of ourselves. We forget the mistakes of others easily but remember our own mistakes forever. We know in theory that if we grant ourselves acceptance and love that we will project to others those same gifts, but we have a hard time practicing this. We are not very gentle with ourselves.

Living in sync with myself is a quest of mine. A quest to accept that I will struggle with allowing life to lead and that I will not always be able to live in a state of softness—that sometimes the sharp edges will appear—and to know that this is not imperfection but soulful growth and understanding.

With absolute conscious effort, I try to find a time each day to be still and stop the noise of life. Sometimes I am successful and in those times I feel a deep contentment and warmth and acceptance of life in all its colors and forms. But when the noise demands to be heard, I must simply be at peace with that part of life, too.

I wish for you this day that you will find a moment without life's noise and that it will bring you closer to practicing the opposite of the well-known verse: Do unto yourself as you would do unto others. Love, accept, and forgive *you*.

WINTER

SOUL SONGS

The dawn creeps ever so slowly and gently across the hilltop. After days of rain and wind, there is stillness here. A few tentative birds begin their song of welcome to the quiet, soggy land. The barren branches of the trees are silhouetted against the light of the early sky, their leaves having flown afar. The glow of holiday lights on the deck is all I write by this morning and there is a peace that prevails—a peace I wish to last all the moments of my day.

When I am with my grandchildren, I know that I am living at the very highest level of human existence. These little people make my soul sing. I am captivated by their innocence, their curiosity, their expression of love, how they learn and live with excitement and wonder. When I consider how much joy I find in them, I recognize that emulating how they live is what I should strive for. To capture these qualities that fill up my soul has been my lifelong goal. There is a lyric from a Martina McBride song that says, "I see who I want to be in my daughter's eyes." There is so much we can learn from children, who are closer to spiritual understanding than we adults. As adults we have too many filters and not enough sincerity—too much acquired knowledge of how to hide our hearts and souls, seeking happiness through just about everything but our own inner self. Children, thankfully, have not yet become so "wise."

Yesterday I watched my mother—fragile, limited in her cognitive skills now—as she watched her great-grandchildren. She asked if she could hold our new little granddaughter and as she cuddled the baby close to her I could almost feel the serenity and homecoming of her heart. The moments my mother is truly happy anymore are rare, but I knew this was one of them. And I knew in that moment my mother was at her highest level of living. I was so grateful to witness this and to be reminded of all the giving and loving my mother has done in her life.

I believe we all have experiences living at that highest level. We should be aware of how we feel when we are there, and why, and then try to bring ourselves to that same place in as many moments as possible. When we feel that kind of lifting of spirit, we know exactly what fills us up. As we move through life, the more moments we live that way and feel that way, the more those moments will return to us. It is our own unique journey—our own expression of who we are and why we live.

For me, watching children nurtures my soulful song. This is my spring in the middle of winter. If I can but capture even one small spark of the inner light my grandchildren share with me, then perhaps I, too, can be a whisper of spring in winter.

SITTING QUIETLY

The day began in a blanket of varying hues of gray. On a sunny dawn, you can close your eyes for a moment and, upon opening them, the view has shifted and changed and warmed. Today, regardless of how many times you closed and opened your eyes, or the minutes in between, the view remained a constant gray. I wasn't, therefore, paying much attention. But in a glance, I was captured by a break in the clouds that was spilling joyous light. It seemed to be calling me—reminding me—that the light is always there.

Each day I have the gift of sitting quietly, alone, with a blanket around my feet and a contented cat on my lap. During this time I slip to the joyous spaces and places of the light in life. The peace is so present, the faith so secure, the bliss so tangible. My soul sighs in pleasure and all things are possible. And then the clock hits 7:00 a.m. and my moment is done. Everyday life begins.

How do I hold on to the gift of sitting quietly the entire day long? I used to envision myself wearing a protective coat of armor that repelled every negative bullet I encountered in my day. The chatter of life—the noise—eventually penetrated the shield and I drifted from that light amidst the clouds to the blanket of gray. This has long been my vision. I read the books about running off to India for months at a time to study and meditate and I wondered how my bank account could ever afford that luxury. Well, it can't. So the real question is how to find the inner light on a daily basis no matter what is zinging around me. It is easy to believe in the positive and the beautiful when you are not trying to live everyday life at the same time.

Some days I am very successful at feeling the strength of the inner light. Some days I am not. All days I live life with the intent of finding the light and the love that fuels its fires. All days I look for the little things that can still make me smile and feel the bliss of sitting quietly if only for a flash of a moment—just like the opening in the clouds—reminders that the light is always there. If I am not paying attention, not watching for those moments, I will miss the opportunity to remember and to keep my balance.

May you feel the light today, if only for a moment, and find comfort in knowing that even in everyday life, the light is always there.

STRONG-WILLED CHILD

The sound of pouring rain on the deck filled the quiet morning. The birds were not awake or singing, the cats were snuggled up in bed. How different my beginnings are these days than just a few months ago when I welcomed the day and the sunshine with the French doors open, the bird orchestra in full melody, and the cats lounging on the deck. The seasons change. Life changes also.

We move along and rather subtly things shift until one day we wake up and realize how different things are today than they were yesterday and how different they are than what we thought they would be. That might be the absolute fascination of life—how it twists and turns and brings us to places that are unexpected and foreign to what we believed life would be, and what we believed we would be.

There is a song written by John Denver that says, "I can see there's a danger in becoming what I never thought I'd be." Now, that change can be a good thing or it can be a not good thing. If we are becoming what we do not wish to be, it is our choice to make changes and evolve in a positive way; then we can click our heels and say "Cool beans!" at what we have become. Life propels us forward and becomes an adventure that is the most well-written, spellbinding tale we will ever know. Stepping back and recognizing how the tale has progressed and moved us becomes a valuable exercise in reflection.

Life is often like the weather. All the measurements and predictions in the world are fooled by the power of the weather, and of life—the epitome of a strong-willed child! The wonder is in what the next day or moment or chapter will bring and how we will choose to live life as it unfolds before us.

INSANITY WORKS

Clouds have obscured the stars for days. The winter nights are inky black and lifeless with the loss of the twinkling heavens to dream upon. Even the moon is hiding. Only the glittering of holiday lights reminds us of the magic above.

Every year since 1988, I have written myself a Christmas letter. It began as a list of what I needed for the next year so I wouldn't forget, and what went well the last year and what didn't work at all, and ideas for how to make things brighter the next year. It evolved into something much more—how life had been that year, how I felt about all that happened, and my hopes and goals for the year ahead.

Each year about this time, I take out my Christmas letters and read them—all of them. Patterns emerge. Patterns of insanity. The definition of insanity is doing the same things over and over again and expecting different results. Ah yes, I do this every year. My letters all say, Try not to do too much, spend too much, eat too much. And each year, with just a few exceptions, I ignore my well-intentioned advice. Perhaps this is simply part of the holiday tradition for me. (Insanity at its finest.)

There have actually been some pretty funny comments in these letters over the years that perhaps others might relate to:

"Kids fought over the Advent calendar. "

"Too much school activity helping."

"Don't sew in December."

"Don't bake like a crazy woman."

"Help husband put up the outdoor lights and give him whiskey. It works better that way."

"Don't push so hard to make it perfect."

"Today is Christmas Day. I feel like the Pillsbury Doughboy."

"Don't buy poinsettias. They always die."

"Hire someone to clean the house." (Noted several years; haven't done it yet.)

"Don't get the Christmas tree in the freezing rain just because it's on the schedule."

"No time to fall asleep on the couch."

"Wrapping at midnight is not a good thing."

And then there are my serious moments, like the last paragraph of my letter to myself last year:

"Let me be older but younger in spirit; wiser but also smarter; let me be firm in my convictions but open to perspectives that are different than my own; less driven but equally as focused; more able to laugh and more able to cry when I need to; let me experience life with delight but remember to be reflective; let me reach within to find the light given to me and reach without to share it fearlessly with others."

As you plan your holiday season, remember that what sounds perfectly doable today will exhaust you by Christmas Eve. If you bake them, you will eat them. If you buy them, you must wrap them. And love truly is the greatest gift of all.

ANGELS

The wind chimes were swinging and singing in the blustery wind. Water was pouring from the overworked gutters and splattering to the deck below like waterfalls on rocks. In the early morning light the trees were rocking and swaying in a frantic exposé of motion. Winter echoes all around us. It was a lovely day to play inside.

It was my day. I had orchestrated this very day for two months. This was my day to wrap presents. Wrapping presents is something I have always loved to do and over the years I have found a way to have just such a day every year at Christmas. There is a fire in the fireplace, the pitch popping merrily; the Christmas music is turned up; all the holiday lights are on despite the daylight; and I'm all by myself. Soon the wrapping paper and perfect ribbon will have my full attention. Sometimes the packages I think will be spectacular do not turn out to be all that special. And sometimes the ones I cannot envision being beautiful turn out to be my very favorites. The unexpected beauties are a special gift. (Pun intended.)

As I sat before my tree and admired the results of my special day nestled beneath the branches, I thought about my recent visit to my best friend, significantly impaired now from illness. My conversations with my wonderful friend remain limited but she is always glad to see me and we talk about something and nothing each visit. This visit was different.

The visit began as it always does and then she asked me to hold her hand. Suddenly she looked at me very intently and stopped talking. She focused on my eyes and I slowly grew to realize it was my soul she was really seeing. I had gone through a sorrowful event in the past week but, being me, I refused to allow it to overtake me. Or perhaps I just refused to acknowledge my pain. She, however, saw my sorrow and would not let go of my hand. She continued to look into my eyes and I felt the tears slip. She held tighter to my hand but said nothing. For twenty minutes this is what we did. I would try to talk but she would not respond. And slowly I began to acknowledge how much I still needed this special friend in my life to know my sorrows and my fears. She was giving me what I needed in spite of her limitations.

I believe we find angels to guide us in unexpected moments and their gifts are so powerful and precious that they change us forever. Sometimes it is not the brush of a wing that touches us, but the grasp of a hand.

SNOWMEN

The evergreens were bowing gracefully in the wind as though they knew this was their season of glory. While most other trees have had their last encore, the tall evergreens spread their green beauty across the nondescript land with a royalty all their own.

Today was one of those days I would define as divine. Clean house (relatively speaking), fire in the fireplace, Christmas lights shining on a foggy morning, Christmas music filling the spaces, and my indoor snowmen awaiting the day upon which they are traditionally placed in the perfect spot for one magical month.

Some of you reading this might say, "Big deal. Snowmen. Whoopee!" I collect snowmen and have over 150 of them. I don't know how that actually happened. I was just drawn to them because they were happy creatures. I don't recall ever seeing a frowning snowperson. And, they are round—I can relate! But somehow I ended up with a very large snowman collection that I display each year and they have become my very special treasures.

As I have received snowmen through the years, I have written on the bottom of each gift the year and the person's name who gave it to me. Each of these snowmen represents a relationship and time in my life, like chapters in a lifelong book. Some of the friends who have given me snowmen have passed away, some are no longer able to participate in this world as they once did, some have drifted to other places and circumstances, and some remain as close as ever. The snowmen are a way for me to remember with warmth and smiles all these people who have played, and continue to play, a significant part in my life.

My snowmen remind me of all those who have been a part of the chapters in my lifelong book, and today, I am grateful for each of them and all they have brought to the pages of who I am. Friendships, like snowmen, are a happy collection of memories and moments I am forever grateful for.

COMFORT AND JOY

The view from my window this morning was a typical winter day. The land was frozen, the vegetation stiff from the frigid air, and the snow lay nestled atop the leaves that had fallen only a few weeks ago. The eastern sky began to glow and the paintbrush of the gods slipped across the clouds in pink and gold. The barren branches of the winter trees were dark against this backdrop. What a perfect winter picture this was.

Our grandson made a fascinating discovery at school last week—Santa's Secret Shop, a place for kids to buy inexpensive presents for family members all by themselves. On the first day of discovery, he spent his popcorn money to buy his mommy a present. He was so excited about this that he brought all his money to his mom when he got home and announced he was going to buy presents for all his family the next day at recess. So, she gave him some extra and off he went with his list and his coffers of cash. Upon arriving home that day, he proudly showed her all his gifts, each in little white sacks with carefully marked tags. The last little white sack boldly sported a tag that read, "To: Me. From: Me." How delightful is that? From the pure innocence of a child, a very significant life lesson: we spend a great deal of energy in life giving to others and often forget the importance of also giving to ourselves. Even more importantly, we forget that it is okay to do so.

In our home at this time of year hang two signs: *Comfort and Joy* and *Be Merry*. Perhaps they should be present all year to remind us of these wise statements. We should live our lives with comfort and joy all year long and not just be reminded of this message in lines of Christmas songs for one month. To give and receive comfort in the moments of our life, and to find joy in everyday things, will make the second sign far easier: *Be merry*. True, sincere merriment provides us the ability to experience laughter and spiritual abundance and minimizes our need to communicate our woes to others. Joy becomes the ever-flowing spring of positive energy and light in our lives and the lives of those around us.

My wish for you this holiday season is that you will seek comfort and joy each day and that in doing so, you will find an abundance of merriment and love amidst the hurry, the scurry, the mundane, the routine, the sometimes troublesome days in life. And every so often, may there be a gift for you bearing the tag: "To: Me. From: Me."

COOKIES AND CRYSTAL

The room was still and warm. Embers from last night's fire still crackled. I was surrounded by the stars of Christmas on the tree, on the deck rail, on the bushes in the front yard. For this moment in time, I paused to appreciate the beauty and the peace of the season. For a few days each year, we capture the essence of the glory of life, snippets of appreciation and love. This is the magic of Christmas.

Have you ever noticed how wonderful cookies taste when served on a crystal plate? A normal cookie suddenly turns into a gourmet delight. Yesterday, after a holiday event, I started to take the lace tablecloth from the table and then I stopped. It was so elegant and pretty. Why was I removing it? I left it there and we ate our hamburger dinner from the china poinsettia plates. Hamburgers never tasted so good! In our practical approach to life, we often forget to transform the mundane to the divine. The little things that turn life into something special are often reserved for when we are in the company of others and then quickly we put them aside so we can return to a more austere style of living. Why do we do that?

I once read that in each task you undertake, you should add a touch that is your soul's signature. I've always liked that thought. I have tried to incorporate that into my daily routines and work. Everyone's soulful touch is different but when you add it to your living, you recognize it, and it feels good. For me, candles and pretty tables, crystal dishes, and flowers and photographs are part of my soulful signature. But even the way you stack your dishes in the cupboard or pack your lunch or sign your name can be a reflection of that as well. It is that personal flourish in how you do things—how you approach life—that captures a piece of you not always visible in our busy world.

We are the masters of finding the joy in everyday life. It is within our power and our control to take normal moments and shift them to a higher place simply by our awareness of and appreciation for the beauty and magic in the simplicity of living. Pausing to notice life as it goes by moves us to that place and fills us moment by moment with what we call happiness.

May you find happiness today in the warmth of a coffee cup in your hands, soft socks on your feet, the heater in your car, the raindrop on your nose, the kiss from a kitty, the smile from a child, the sound of the washing machine, the clicking of computer keys, warm water in the shower, and cookies from a crystal tray.

RUM BALLS

The distant hills, high against the warming sky, were a deep, frosty blue with snow dust upon them. A December morning, stark, cold, and beautiful still in this barren season. As the sun began to slide across the hilltops, it spilled winter light across the landscape. Winter light is different than light in other seasons. It is simplistic and sharp and reveals more without the complexities of leaves to absorb and reflect its light.

At this time of year, I am acutely aware of one of my basic personality flaws. That flaw would be having unrealistic expectations about what one person can do in any given period of time. I love the holiday season but it exhausts me. I could "not do" but I want to "do." I find myself making multiple lists and checking each one more than twice. We push two months of activity into a three-week time period, which doesn't leave room for lingering. Or does it? Do we have a conscious choice to "take five"?

In the past, I have attempted to minimize the rush of the season by delegating my to-do list to my husband, but it doesn't always turn out as the planner had planned. Women must be sensitive about their spouses' engagement in the holiday activities. Assuming they do *not* want to engage can be a misstep, but assuming they *will* engage is equally as dangerous and can result in a spirited discussion about which one of you makes Christmas happen.

A few years ago I tentatively asked my husband if he would like to help me with any of the Christmas shopping. Knowing he may be on unsteady ground, he paused for a while and then carefully said, "I'm not too big into shopping." That was actually the right answer. Whew! He did, however, suggest that we make rum balls and eagerly volunteered to assist me as he believed his expertise would be valuable as to how much rum should go into these delicacies. Encouraged by his willingness to participate in the holiday tradition of baking, I eagerly accepted his offer.

So we ventured into the land of rum balls and my husband put so much rum in them that we had to add dry ingredients three times before we could roll them into balls. (That's okay. I could be tolerant of this oversight since *he* had been tolerantly eating dinner off of snowman plates for the past few weeks.) As I was cleaning up the dishes, I asked him if he would put the second coat of powdered sugar on the rum balls and showed him how to drop the ball into the sack of powdered sugar and shake it. I went busily about my task, not really paying attention to him. Then I heard him say, "These are sure a pain in the butt" and looked up. There was powdered sugar everywhere—all over the counter like fine dust, all over his hands, his shirt, his nose, his moustache, and even his glasses! I thought I would die laughing—I could not contain myself. Perhaps all the rum had not gone into those rum balls after all.

Since then, we have not repeated the rum ball exercise. He just drinks the rum and forgets the ball part of the recipe. He lingers, I rush. It's our tradition.

TRUDGING

There was no lure of fine, soft weather to walk in this morning. I had to force myself to don my coat, my gloves, my scarf wrapped tightly over my head, and extend a foot, then another, into the damp chill of the outside air. The ground was soggy. Puddles stood openly, daring a foot to find a path around them. Leaves that were left upon the trees were brown, dangling and wet. It was not the pleasant trip about the hilltop of warmer days.

Concentrating on putting one foot in front of the other, I trudged along the road even though I so wanted to return to the warmth of my home. I knew that returning to where I had been was not the right thing to do. Walking clears my head and my heart. I needed to feel the wind on my face, the cold of my jeans against my legs, and to observe the day from nature's perspective. So, I kept going. One step at a time. And I started to daydream about tulips, daffodils, and bright blue spring skies. I remembered in vivid detail the warm winds of summer and the chattering of the birds. I forgot I was trudging.

We all go through periods of time when our life resembles winter. When we just are not in happy sync with what is happening around us or within us. We seem to be one step off in our dance with life. Our toes are being stepped on and we miss the turns. Certainly the dips are not graceful. They hurt our back! During those times, we must just put one foot in front of the other. We must simply keep moving, knowing that winter does not last forever—it just feels that way sometimes. And we must not think about the trudging. We need to focus forward on the returning sun when our feet will skip in time to the music of easier times.

In the dark, dreary times of the year, we need to be kind to ourselves. Take the opportunity to be still, to be quiet inside, to nurture yourself with patience and tolerance for the uncertainty of the moment. Have faith that the flowers will return. It is the way of life. It is the magic of life.

CRANBERRY BLISS

For days the fog clung to the frozen earth, its gossamer blanket turning the trees to frosty wonders, held captive by the frigid mist. Through the fog came the wind, tossing the blanket aside, bringing sunshine to cold air, finding every crack and crevice, and sending the birds and creatures to silent places of protection. Today the wind stopped. In the perfect stillness, the birds twittered and sang, distant dogs barked, and nature sighed with relief. If one closed their eyes, it would seem a summer day except for the stark cold air that slipped across the skin.

Last Christmas I discovered Cranberry Bliss Bars at Starbucks. Divine! I waited all year for them to arrive again. I knew what day they were coming and made sure I was there to partake of this bliss. Then I found a copycat recipe on the internet for these sinful, delightful pleasures and I made a whole pan of them—twice. Yesterday I told my husband that I was never making them again and he looked at me rather oddly. I explained that I wanted to just go to Starbucks once or twice during the season and experience the magic with a great cup of coffee. By having them so accessible, the bliss had disappeared and I felt robbed of the pleasure.

We rob ourselves of the bliss sometimes because we forget to savor the delightful things in life. I do not advocate a life of deprivation but a life of "experiential savoring." I used to drink my coffee black. Then one day I started to have cream and sugar only on Saturdays as a treat. Heaven! The next step was to have cream and sugar in my coffee when I was traveling as a reward for getting up at 3:00 a.m. to make the trek to the airport. Somehow that turned into having cream and sugar in my coffee every day and the joy was no longer the same. Now, in this case, giving up my cream and sugar so that I can practice savoring is not an option. No way! However, this morning I made a conscious effort to appreciate the sweetness and the warmth as I sipped. I was grateful to move from precious sleep to awareness with this treat in my hands as I began my day.

Bliss is about taking the moments we have doing things we love and truly experiencing them rather than rushing through them or taking them for granted. Too much of a good thing, and we stop appreciating them. Sometimes we move too fast to stop and be part of a single moment of gratitude for something we love. Savor life. *Remember* to savor life and make the decision to do so.

May we have the wisdom to know when we are taking the bliss out of the Cranberry Bliss Bars in all aspects of life.

NEW BEGINNINGS

Torrents of water poured from the skies today, creating streams of muddy water down the gravel road and subduing the squirrels and birds hiding in their protected places. It felt cold and wet everywhere. Suddenly the rain stopped and for a mere moment the sun peeked through the dark clouds and painted a rainbow across the winter sky. A reminder that the magic of spring was in the making, though winter was all around us.

Winter. January. New beginnings. Resolutions. Yesterday I began a new exercise program and a new commitment to ban the added weight of holiday bliss bars from my thighs. I even hired a personal trainer to help me incorporate toning and strengthening exercises to my more peaceful yoga routine. Today I am so stiff and sore I am moving as though I were thirty years older and I'm "chugging" carrots to keep from eating sugar straight from the sugar bowl. This feels more like insanity than progress!

I admire people with strong discipline about diet and exercise; I just find it a struggle to mimic them. Donning workout wear is a little daunting if you ever have to leave the accepting space of your home. I'm working out for a reason and it isn't because I look smashing in sweats and T-shirts! And, are my movements smooth and energetic when I get there? Well, let's just say that the Pilates tape I bought a few years ago turned into a laughing fest in the middle of my living room. And I was alone!

Dieting is much like seeking a deeper spiritual lifestyle. In both cases we are required to change habits—habitual ways of eating or habitual ways of thinking. We get off to a great start and as long as life is running smoothly we do very well with the theories we apply. Then life gets bumpy and suddenly we are struggling to convert theory into reality. We fall so easily back into the ways in which we are comfortable, the ways that feel familiar when life is uncertain or stressful. Knowing what we should or should not eat is one thing—building that into our daily lives is a totally different skill set. Making it happen in real life is my quest, in spite of the everyday strains and stresses that slip in and out of life.

I have a stack of diet books about three feet high. I have a stack of spiritual enlightenment books about twice that high. Absorbing knowledge does not, however, make you wise, spiritual, or thin. Living life and making the journey on our own is how we grow. A wonderful mentor of mine once said, "Remember that your mentors are not always right." Even our mentors have their own paths. We must find our own way, according to our own life experience, to become all that we can and wish to be.

I love the days when I am serene and carrots are my friend. On the other days, I am simply grateful for the delightful soul who first created chocolate cake.

ICY BUTTERFLIES

The snow is falling lightly from the sky today, like confetti from heaven. It drifts upon the air with the lightness of an icy butterfly, swirling and playing in its journey with no hindrance or thought. The snow creates a scene of serenity on a cold, rather barren winter land.

We all have an enormous power that we seldom consider. In fact, it may be the greatest power of any human and it occurs in an instant without any effort. It is called a smile. Have you ever considered the impact of a single smile? For the billions of dollars spent on teaching excellent customer service, and the monumental efforts of organizations everywhere to promote positive employee and customer relations, the simple smile is perhaps the most effective resource and strategy in the world and it is free.

There has rarely been a time in my life when a smile that spontaneously escapes my lips is not reciprocated. Eyes grow warm, connections are made, and life around us is better. Smiles should not be reserved just for the people you know, but for all people. It is a universal language of mankind. Tears are, too, though I prefer smiles. We, as a species, want solutions for connecting teams, companies, and countries to one another; how often we forget the tools we are born with that already connect us naturally. Yes, I know it is much more complicated than that, but think about it for a moment. A smile tells us so much about someone else. We know a smile is real if it "reaches their eyes"—we never have to speak a word. A smile opens doors, it breaks down barriers, it touches hearts, and it sends warmth to the person who smiles and to the receiver. A smile is a magical phenomenon that we experience every day.

I received a quote the other day from a friend. This quote was buried in one of those forwarded e-mails that seem to go on and on, but it caught my attention because it was so true: "Don't frown. You never know who is falling in love with your smile." What a great observation!

REACHING OUT

A soft dusting of fresh snow lay quietly, bringing an unusual loveliness to the starkness of the land. All the hidden intricacies of every branch and blade were suddenly brought into full view. The purity of the air, the purity of the white world, surrounded me, enveloped me, and gave me a sense of newness and serenity.

A swift wind had come through the woods a few days before, leaving broken limbs scattered all about. It was not possible to walk without my feet stepping on them. I looked up to see if I could spot the damage in the trees but their needles obscured the wounds of the wind. I thought about the branches on the trees, how vulnerable the tree would be without them. The branches, reaching out through the air, gave the tree more stability and protection than a simple trunk rising straight up could ever provide. While the trunk is the core strength of the tree, without the branches to balance and nourish the core, the tree would perish. This reaching out is important.

Reaching out is also important for humans. If we extend our hearts and souls to others, if we embrace new ideas and thoughts, if we stretch beyond the limitations imposed upon us over years of external messaging, we, too, will have a stronger core. It is true that when we reach out, there is the risk that people and events will hurt us just as the wind pruned the branches from the trees. Yet without extending ourselves to others and other ideas in life, we will not grow and thrive. We will not learn the songs of our life just as the trees cannot whisper in the wind without branches to carry the song. Our relationships and our willingness to experience life must include reaching out beyond ourselves.

The difference between nature and humans is that humans have been given a choice as to how they grow and experience life. Trees grow where they are planted and if they are not thriving they are not given the choice to get up and move. They must flourish where they are, regardless of the circumstances. Humans, however, have the ability to make changes that will allow them to thrive and flourish beyond their current circumstances.

The gift of choice is so significant. Accept it, nurture it, and celebrate it. The trees reach out wherever they are to gain strength and balance. We can reach out whenever we choose to find the same.

COVEY MOMENT

It was very cold and very dark. I left the warmth and comfort of my home in the early morning hours, heading to the airport to catch a plane that would carry me far away. Few cars were on the streets and all the world seemed a bit lonely. Amidst the winter chill appeared twinkling lights, leftovers from Christmas that someone could not yet banish to the tubs and bins and boxes of holiday décor. Here and there I spotted them as I drove and I was struck by how much cheer and warmth they brought to the darkness around them. My car was warm, and the occasional brightness of these lights made my beginning to a long week so much better. I was grateful for this moment and the small tokens of celebration still gracing the world in the bleakness of winter.

Riding the elevator up to my room in the hotel, I was struck by all the busyness swirling around me in anticipation of the meeting I was attending. And, there was a small moment of recognition that none of it really mattered, though we all pretended it did. How often we engage in this rather shallow busyness of life. As Stephen Covey has written, spending time on the urgent and not on the important is what really matters. While Covey's principle has mostly been applied to business, I believe it also applies to life in general. The "urgent" becomes all those things that demand our time and our mind on a daily basis and if we live there all the time, we lose the "important" more and more. We need to focus on the "important" in life which is the heart and soul—relationships, love, faith, and grace. We often shove them aside to meet deadlines and forge ahead in our careers and activities. However, if we were to stop working tomorrow, or if a significant health issue or threatening life circumstance occurred for us or someone we love, all of this "urgency" would vanish from our focus immediately. I find it fascinating that the human species is so easily distracted from the "important" in life.

I enjoy my work. I believe in the mission of the company and the people who form this company. I know that working in my profession allows me the opportunity to engage my mind in these tasks of "urgency" and opens doors for me to touch others with what is "important." I just believe that we need to recognize urgency as a temporary circumstance and put it in perspective when we are running wild with "urgent" on our mind. By recognizing this, we take a step back, even for only a moment, and enjoy a calmer clarity to our day. This takes us to a more peaceful, accepting place that guides us more surely through the busyness.

My recognition of the busyness on the elevator was not unlike the bright lights twinkling in the deep darkness of a winter morning, reminding me of the joy and celebration of life amidst the activity and commotion of everyday living; reminding me to stay in touch with the important in spite of the urgent.

ICY PINNACLES

After days of a bone-chilling east wind, the morning air was calm and still. A few birds were singing with appreciation and enthusiasm for at last being able to glide rather than perform arduous aerobics to make their way against the wind. The sun was shining, though it seems lately as reluctant to rise into the cold winter air as we are, staying low in the southernmost sky all day until it slips under the blanket of darkness once again. Ground water lies stiff in icy patches where it last flowed freely and from the earth have risen fragile pinnacles of ice where water once resided. Along the banks of ditches and atop the molehills are wondrous structures of icicles standing straight and tall or gracefully bent like grass, bringing to our focus all the spaces and places where the water was hiding unseen. Although it was a frozen day, I could smell the earth from branches that had broken and leaves swept and unsettled by the harsh winds. January was here.

The ice pinnacles made me think about how we must focus to see what usually goes unnoticed when we are consumed with other things. We see only what is in our current view, our current focus. We can become so absorbed in what we are doing or feeling that anything outside of that view seemingly does not exist. We are taught—commanded—to focus on what we are doing from a very young age. Focus is generally thought of as a positive trait. And when we focus too much on something, then we are called obsessive. I cannot decide if the art of focusing is limiting or freeing. Perhaps it is both.

Focus is a very powerful human ability. We comprehend so little of how magnificent our minds are. When something moves our focus, a whole new perspective opens up to us. If we give something our full attention, often the very same thing occurs. The ice pinnacles show us that the water that moves along the earth is always there, but we seldom see it or acknowledge it until it turns to a very tangible form. It is always there for our knowing but we just don't see it because our focus is on other things.

I wonder how many amazing things surround us that we miss because we are so focused on the tasks and tribulations of life. I am grateful this day for those icy wonders that made me realize how much more there is to see in this lifetime by shifting my focus to a greater awareness of all that is. May we find a way each day to focus on something new outside of our thoughts and worries so that we might discover a new world.

RESPONSE

The sky was austere and cold, a subtle hue of perfection but without warmth. Even the blackberries, which persist in spite of the odds of winter, huddled closer to the ground. Bird nests, once safely hidden, are visible amongst the branches of the tall maples and leafless underbrush. The birds who remain for the winter find their shelter and safety deep within the blackberries and I am forced to admit I have found another element of goodness in this obnoxious plant species with its prickly stems and voracious need to take over the land. It is time to go within for the warmth the outside world does not offer.

I have pondered for some time the value of a response. Let's face it—we are a pretty self-absorbed species, and while each of us absolutely craves a response from the people around us, we often do not give a response to others. We are a needy lot! If you think about it, there is a thrill within us when someone truly notices and pays attention to us. Most of the time we all run franticly through our days, focused on how the world impacts *us*. And we feel unappreciated and unloved when those around us don't respond to *us*. Neil Diamond proclaimed in a song, "'I am,' I cried. 'I am,' said I." Only sometimes we feel we are just saying it to ourselves and no one else really hears.

A response from others is extremely important. I believe many of our behaviors come from the lack of others responding to who we are. Certainly I see this in business, but I also see it in everyday life. When we are first in love, or are still adorable little children, we receive incredible responses that are heady, delicious, and sublime. We then spend most of our time trying to recapture that feeling. *Someone please notice who I am and make me feel that I matter!* People often go to great lengths to receive a response. If you think about the violence and negativity we experience in our world, many times it is driven by someone needing a response—any response. *Just notice who I am!*

Is it simple to respond to others? In a world propelled by activity and demands, it does not seem so. Yet the most successful people—both personally and professionally—respond to others often. I suppose true enlightenment means being so serene within that you do not need a response from the outside world, but very few achieve this. Our human experience is greatly impacted by the response we receive from the world around us.

Today I will remember to respond to the people in my life. Perhaps it will make a difference to someone who needs to feel noticed and heard. I am certain that doing so will make a difference in my own view of the world.

WINTER SPIKES

The breath of nature was very quiet this day, still wrapped in a blanket of winter clouds with just a hint of the sun peeking from behind them. Sleepy. Upon close observation, tiny closed buds of new life were visible upon barren tree limbs, just a hint of a spike that promises the rebirth of green adornment in several weeks' time.

It is the middle of January. By human calculations, winter has just begun. By nature's standards, spring is here. It began, perhaps, the very day we proclaimed it winter. Beneath the cold, often frozen earth, the bulbs are already sprouting and growing; we just can't see them yet. The warmth of life is spreading up through the trees, cautiously and surely, awaiting the exact moment to burst into view.

What we humans often forget is this miracle—this phenomenon—of life is moving even when we, with our limited view, cannot see it. We forget this about nature and we forget this about ourselves. We proclaim our life in a state of winter when things seem to be going sideways, when plans fail, when we simply cannot find the warmth within or the spirit to declare that life is good. We fail to remember that even in this place, we are moving to warmer times. There is growth for us even when life seems to be on hold and out of our grasp. I think it is easier for nature to have this faith than us. We yearn for spring, for signs of spring, and are discouraged when our focus does not bring it into view. Understood. But can we shift our focus? Can we find our faith? The answer, I believe, we all possess but must find for ourselves. Sometimes I think we can't begin to find it if we don't experience the winter. Only in looking back do we see how it was there all the time and we simply missed it.

I am grateful today for the quiet of nature so that I could see life beginning to form on the trees and remember the birth that occurs even as winter begins. This new life gave me faith for my own, faith that spring will arrive gloriously as planned.

HUMAN REGIMENT

It is warmer today. All the winter life above the surface is flowing freely and breathing with ease again. The ice has turned to moving masses of puddles and full ditches and the trees are swaying like dancers rather than with the stiffness of soldiers. An almost audible sigh of pleasure is present in nature in this moment of warmth in the midst of the winter chill. The birds are eating heartily to sustain the winter elements of January while humans everywhere are starving themselves to meet their New Year's resolution. During the time when we need comfort food the most, we deprive ourselves of it. Like the stiffness of nature on icy days, we move with controlled effort.

It is amazing, really, how much we humans attempt to control. I count calories, count money, count time. I live from budgets, calendars, clocks, lists, and strategic plans. I have schedules for morning, noon, and night. I know exactly what day to grocery shop, do the laundry, and dust. Often we are just living life stiff. Feeling the pleasure of nature this morning, and knowing that I was not tightening against the cold and the wind as I walked, made me wonder why we do not feel the flow of life more. Our human regimented ways inhibit our ability to sway with life.

As a very organized person, I have been teased about not

being spontaneous enough. There is truth to that for sure, but I guess it depends on your definition of spontaneous. I find spontaneity in the tiniest moments of time: the crackle of the fire, the wind against my cheeks, the feel of soft socks on my feet and tightly tied shoes, the smell of the shampoo in the shower, the beauty of a single blossom, the warmth of a kiss, the pat from a tiny hand, the first sip of a fine wine, the way the light from the lamp on a dark night, the sound of raindrops, and the taste of snowflakes. In microseconds I am transported from organized to spontaneous. The control slips away, and I allow myself to remember the flow of life lives.

I do not advocate abandoning the human need for control. It seems imperative that some organization exist in order for us to survive in our world. But to *thrive* in our world we need to make a conscious effort to feel the flow and experience the ease of heart, mind, and soul that comes when we allow ourselves to move more freely with life. Living stiff makes us old before our time and impedes our ability to smile on the inside. We miss the tiny moments that are the foundation to our happiness.

So perhaps I will eat macaroni and cheese for dinner tonight rather than salad and enjoy every moment of my day's allotted caloric intake. This will, however, inhibit the flow of the zipper on my jeans.

SNOWFLAKES

Snowflakes were drifting down from the heavens. The hush only experienced on snowy mornings filled the spaces of the earth around me. Softly, surely, the land became pure, white, and renewed. In moments, the magic of life was visible to all.

I am always reminded when it snows of the infinite power of the universe. If you consider that there are no two snowflakes alike, and how many snowflakes actually fall, you cannot help but be awed by this magnificence. If this is true, it is simply not possible for humankind to truly comprehend the forces that surround us daily from powers we only experience in whispers. How then can we not challenge ourselves to believe in miracles and dreams that appear impossible but exist around us every day?

Our limitations certainly exist. Will we become totally enlightened beings who soar through life every day with absolute understanding and peace? Some, perhaps, can achieve this but most of us are here to experience life—not necessarily master it. However, I believe if we are open to those infinite possibilities we will always see life as the magical adventure it is; that we will always find the moments to be awed and amazed at what is all around us.

Only yesterday I paused for a minute and happened to look down at the moss growing profusely on the bank of the ditch. I look at moss all the time but I don't really see it. This day I knelt down for a closer view and was astonished to find that each clump of moss is composed of hundreds of tiny, star-like entities that are as delicate and graceful as any vegetation you will find. Instead of seeing a green clump that flourishes in many places I would rather it didn't, I now viewed moss as a thing of beauty. We have a tendency to view people in much the same way. But by shifting our view, taking that moment to step a little closer, we often find that there is a unique, delicate beauty that we may have missed.

I do not possess the capacity to live life in awareness and euphoria each day. I do possess the capacity to capture it in moments. Every moment I do capture it, my ability to know joy and love and appreciation for all of life expands. I am grateful today for the snowflakes that grace the land and remind us of all we are and can be in this infinite experience of life.

SQUIRRELS

With hands deep in my pocket, I trudged a bit cautiously over frozen ground. There was a dusting of snow across the land I love and a stillness only experienced when the air is frigid and clear. My feet crunching on the cold, icy gravel echoed across the hilltop. The winter sun was rising brilliantly in the eastern sky, light shimmering across the earth. Cold as it was, I welcomed the rays upon my cheeks and stood for a moment, basking in the glow. The sun was the same sun as summer, but how different the landscape today than only a few months ago.

One of the luxuries of living in the country amongst the trees is that you are able to toss things over the hill that nourish the earth as the underbrush takes it into its fold. One day I happened to look up at a very large fir tree and noticed something bright yellow stuck in the crook of a branch. As I looked closer, I discovered it was a gourd. Some resourceful squirrel had happened upon the discarded gourd and, thinking it was a new gourmet delight, carried it up the tree only to learn it was not what he expected. So he abandoned the gourd in this unexpected place and provided me with a chuckle.

I was watching the squirrels outside my window this morning and laughing at their antics. They are like monkeys scampering through the trees with lightning speed and agility, chattering to each other. Up close, they race around the tree with the squirrel feeder on it, fighting and scrabbling as though they were king of the peanuts. (Yes, we feed the squirrels, for in our neighborhood they are not invasive or destructive—just amusing.) Although it is winter, these squirrels are round and plump, certainly not starving, yet they battle over their position at the feeder as though they had not had sustenance for days, even though a power larger than they replenishes the feeder daily with plenty of nourishment for them all. There are "older soul" squirrels that come later to taste the peanuts and they do not need to barter and bash for them, as the crowd has dissipated. But the feeder still has peanuts.

The squirrels rather remind me of humans. We have become a scampering and chattering species. We, too, grab what we think is the gourmet ingredient in life and often discover it is not what we expected, abandoning it to find something else to fill the empty space. We race around the corporate trees, scrabbling and fighting for position and power, as though our very life depends on the perceived sustenance we will receive from being first at the feeder of life, allowing no others nourishment. We forget, or are unknowing, that a power larger than us replenishes the "feeder" daily and that there is more than enough goodness for everyone. The race for survival does not need to be a race at all if we have the knowledge and the faith that what we require in life will be provided every day. It is the power of the belief that sustains us rather than the peanuts we scrabble for.

I watch the squirrels in fascination. They make me wonder if whoever is watching us does so with the same admiration, amusement, and amazement at our antics of living.

SOUTHWEST WINDS

As I stepped into the outside world today, the smell of tilled nature greeted me. It was the same aroma as freshly tilled dirt in the late spring, earthy, deep, sweet—yet it was January! A harsh east wind had been blowing for days, pruning the trees and tossing the foliage about without mercy. This tilling of the forest is what assailed my senses and for a moment sent me slipping into warmer, gentler times. I found it fascinating that the same aroma occurred from this windy thrashing as from moving the soil. I wonder if richness and depth come to all of life on earth when balance is redefined.

In our part of the country, the east wind comes blowing relentlessly for days at a time. It is either hot or cold and never lets up. One wonders how it can just keep blasting away without taking a breath. It is actually quite annoying. Even the cats don't like it. The wind puts a zapping current in the air that leaves the animals wary of touch and wears down the human spirit with its endless huffing. Once it finally departs, it takes the trees and foliage days to relax and stand tall again.

The southwest wind, on the other hand, blows in spurts with a more gentle hand that reminds us of the power behind the wind but does not hammer away for days. Generally, it is only hours and refreshes the landscape and then casually bows away from our world. While it can bring strong rains and, on occasion, show its force, it has a softer touch than the harping east wind. The trees and foliage whip about in its presence but once it departs, stand tall and relax immediately.

People often emulate these winds. Some come storming in and stay in our face relentlessly, nagging at us, correcting us, commanding us, picking at life constantly, sending everyone on edge with their harshness and snapping; it takes days for people to relax after they are gone. Others react more like the southwest wind, powerful but gentler, directing us, mentoring us, inspiring us, reminding us of their force yet allowing us to breathe and respond. They make their point, then they quietly depart, leaving us renewed and willing to stand tall.

I love the winds from the southwest.

WINTER PEARLS

The snowberries are clinging to the empty branches of the bushes. They grace the gray path along the driveway like pearls scattered from the hand of nature. Fog settles upon the treetops and sifts down in trails of misty haze to the earth below. An occasional ray of sunlight glances off dew-laden limbs with startling brilliance and then fades. Small reminders buried in the winter hues that wonder and beauty still exist.

The snowberries are a reminder that pearls of learning and wisdom are strewn about in the most unusual circumstances—circumstances that might seem void of any ability to teach us something significant and wonderful. Yet if we look back on our lives, we will find that this has happened to us over and over again. Have you ever noticed how traumatic events bring out the goodness in others? How many times friends and relatives suddenly appear for us wearing love on their sleeve when we are unexpectedly faced with an incredible need for the hands of others? Having spent time in the healthcare industry, I have watched the best in people in these moments of great anxiety and fear. It seems to naturally flow from them without restriction. We grow soulfully deeper in the moment the generosity of spirit occurs, even if the generosity does not endure beyond it. And a pearl has been placed in our life in the most challenging of times. It is the knowledge that goodness resides within, a glimpse of the true nature of humanity.

I hope that we can see the pearls without a traumatic event to provide us that view. At the very least I hope the luster remains with us long after the difficult times so that we might nurture it and remember the goodness in good times or bad. The hardest moments in life teach us to reach for the greatest joys. And if we do, we will find them.

PUZZLE PIECES

It was a very cold morning. The cats refused to go outside. The birds were not yet awake. I didn't want to be either. I glanced sleepily out the window. Hanging in the western sky was a beautiful, luminescent full moon waiting to slip below the horizon like a globe of cool light. I stood for just a moment and felt the magnificence before I returned to waking up.

In January and February, my husband and I become puzzle maniacs. We set up a table in front of the warm woodstove and embark with sheer delight on a puzzle journey. Puzzles consume your mind so that you do not think about anything else in life except how to find that next piece that will carry the puzzle forward to completion. Puzzles are very therapeutic.

Last night we began a new puzzle and completed the outside perimeter. As I walked by the table this morning, I noticed that the perimeter was gone. There, all over the floor, were the individual puzzle pieces. Our work had been destroyed by feline saboteurs. We were going to have to start all over. I was frustrated, but then I laughed. How life is like that sometimes. We think we have all the pieces put together and then suddenly, we have to start over. We could toss the pieces back in the box and say forget it, I suppose, but that is not what we will do. That is not what we do in life either.

There have been so many analogies comparing life and business to the pieces in a puzzle; I hesitate to even go there. But this *is* the way our lives progress. We put the basic structure of our lives together and then we begin to fill in the pieces. We focus so intently on that one piece we need to find that we don't see any of the other pieces surrounding us. And many times, no matter how easy it would seem to find an odd-shaped, obvious piece, we search and search and can't find it. Eventually we move on to another quest, and bam! There is that elusive piece we could not see before, so obvious that we wonder how we could have missed it. Is that not just totally how it is with life sometimes? We focus and search and yearn for that missing element that seems to prevent us from moving forward, but we cannot see. Maybe we can't see it because it isn't really the next piece of the puzzle we need to find. Maybe we are so locked into our vision of what the piece should look like that we can't see what it does look like.

Puzzles are a tangible exercise in shifting perspectives—in seeing things in a different way. They remind us of how our perceptions can distort what we do or do not see. Maybe when we just can't seem to find the next piece in the puzzle of life, we need to close our eyes and let a new vision move in front of us, and to be open to the fact that it might be the exact piece we need but it might look very different than we expected. I am a planner and an organized one at that. These can be wonderful traits, but they have their limitations. I usually have a pretty definite idea of how things should look and be. I often have to step back from my expectations—particularly when they aren't fulfilled—and recognize that things are just fine the way they turned out. In fact, often they are better than my restricted view was. It is a continual effort to recognize what we impose on ourselves and a conscious choice to step back and see life differently.

Tonight we will pick up the pieces and start over. And if the cats sabotage our puzzle again, we will take that as a message and throw the pieces back in the box!

CHIN COVERS

The cold, penetrating northeast wind has been ever present the past month. It is an opportunist wind, finding every opening imaginable to share its frigid message with us. A washed-out winter sun slants through the barren trees from a southern angle, mingling in the late afternoon with the wisps of gathering fog in the valley and creating sunsets against the blue of the horizon in hues of faded gold and coral and magenta. The winter moon hangs in the northwestern sky with the same glowing impact as the harvest moon on autumn evenings. It is a bleak light that does not reveal the life beginning to flow beneath the harshness of the ground and the stark branches of the trees. We have absolute faith that spring is beginning to awaken deep within nature's soul. If only we could approach our own lives with this faith during times of darkness.

On Valentine's Day, my husband and I celebrated our wedding anniversary. This significant day also gave me some time to reflect on the things about my husband that I take for granted—little things that I scarcely notice now but if they were gone, I would mourn them. Each morning when I kiss him good-bye there is the slight taste of toothpaste on his lips; each evening when I welcome him home I smell the familiar scent on his flannel shirt of his day at the pattern shop. I would miss his shoes in the kitchen by the furnace register, the fine whiskers in the sink, his socks outside the hamper because he missed the shot, mountains of maps beside his chair, maybe even his old jacket with the duct tape holding it together. (Or not.) I would also miss our nightly cover battle. My husband is a night owl and comes to bed after me. I pull the covers to my chin. He sticks them under his arms. So when he comes to bed he disturbs my chin covers and I have to hang onto them for dear life. I would miss how he never knows to stop petting the cat when the ears go flat and the tail flicks, how he hates little forks and decaffeinated coffee. We find comfort and security in the little things in life and we often fail to appreciate them.

Being married for so many years is a nice place to be. Spring is coming, the days are getting longer. May the little things in life sustain us while we wait.

GOSSAMER PATHS

The sun slipped easily over the horizon, spilling the light of hope upon the trees and hills. The few clouds clinging low turned peach, moving softly across the clear, creamy blue sky of winter. Through the trees, the light came to the earth in streams, like gossamer paths back to the glorious globe that had not been visible for weeks. The birds were everywhere, their songs stronger than I had heard for quite some time. Perhaps they had always been strong but my focus on the rain, wind, and cold had prevented me from hearing them as I did today. Nature had given the earth a break.

Through the bumpy times in our lives, we often use the phrase "Just give me a break!" We yearn for some sign that tomorrow will bring the sunshine back to us. Sometimes it is even hard for us to remember what it looks like or how it feels. While nature receives its break from the warmth of the sun, we find it in the warmth of kindness, thoughtfulness, and love. We also find the inspiration and message of hope in our awareness of the small messages that fall upon us even in difficult times. Awareness is a significant factor in being able to feel hope and keep our faith that the sun still shines for us.

This is why I believe that kindness is so important in our lives. We can be the message—the sun—that slips into the life of another to remind them that love prevails and that tomorrow will show them a brightness that might be lacking today. Handing them the gift of caring is a supreme expression of the divine. We do not need to spend all our time thinking about, or planning, how we can bring this gift to others. It is just part of how we live and it is in the spontaneous smile or encouraging word that we bring this sincere and serene part of ourselves into tangible form. These small acts generate the light from within us and create the gossamer path that connects us to those around us.

It was a true pleasure to feel the sun on my face this day. How little faith I have sometimes, though the world continues to provide all the reminders I need that the sunlight is ever present. I am grateful for the sunshine today and all the gossamer paths that arrive in my life at the most unexpected, most needed, moments.

YEARNING FOR YELLOW

The dawn was without color today. The gray of the morning sky faded into the gray hues of the earth. Brown tinges, dark green needles melding into the fog. This is a season devoid of color, leaving me yearning for yellow.

Today was a terrific day: I found daffodils at the store. Daffodils are my absolute favorite flower, and even though they are just beginning to peek out of their earthy beds outside, they now grace my table with their yellow heads held high like royalty. How can you not feel a sense of hope just knowing their relatives will soon be shining and bobbing in our yard?

Each morning I sit on my couch with the blanket tucked neatly around me like a cocoon, a cup of coffee in my hand, and a kitty on my lap, and I watch for the sun to hint that it is in the sky. This is my cherished time of day. All is still and peaceful. Tranquil. And then, my errant mind begins its incessant chatter. Each day I work very hard at keeping it still, but it is as disobedient as a puppy or a two-year-old child and as persistent as one as well.

Our minds are pretty amazing things but they don't know when to quit. They are incredibly masterful at manipulation and powerful at pulling us into the spin of thinking. My mind wanders quickly to what I need to do that day, what I'm going to wear, how I can approach this part of my life or that, how the kids are, why I have big feet, who wrote that song, the diets I've tried, the triumphs I hope for, the vacation I'm planning and why it will never happen, where my husband's errant sock went, what is that horrible squeak in the car, what if the plane crashes next week, what do I need to remember to take out for dinner, what will I do if my mom falls again . . . You get the idea. And it just goes on and on, random and unrelated and totally not focused. My mind especially likes to slip in to tell me the rules of life and why I can't change them. Sometimes it plays this cat-and-mouse game by thrilling me with possibilities and then dashing them in the next second with doubts. My mind is addicted to judgment.

When my children were very small I would occasionally have a day when the constant conversation and questions and demands would find me slipping off the edge of patience. On rare occasions, I was known to lock myself in the bathroom and remind myself to breathe. These moments lasted about five minutes but gave me the rest I needed to be a good mommy again. I feel the same way sometimes about my mind. Love it, cherish it, appreciate it, but my poor inner self just reaches its limit sometimes and shouts, *Stop! Just stop. I need to hear silence, I need to be. I want you, dear mind, to take a time-out.*

And it listens. For about five seconds. I must be very firm with it when my soul needs the peace of not thinking. The non-stop whys, wherefores, and what-ifs our minds project to us daily can be detrimental to a soulful life if we do not exert our authority over their constant ramblings and musings. There are moments when we just need to take a rest.

May you find five minutes today with an obedient mind that listens to your soul before jumping in with edits and suggestions. It will be a glorious five minutes!

COATS WITH HOLES

I did not want to walk today. The wind felt cold through my jacket, finding every open crevice with its searing power. Each step seemed to make me colder. I kept walking. With the movement, I slowly began to feel warmer. The wind felt friendlier, my motion was smoother, and I began to think of positive things rather than focusing on the harshness of the wind. I was grateful I could move like this, feel the wind itself, and that I was walking on the hilltop in the dawn of a new day. Life was good. Moving through life warms us, albeit slowly sometimes.

My thoughts took me to life and how important it is for us to keep moving even on the days we do not want to do so. Mondays, for instance, always take a little more time, a little more coffee, as we start feeling the "cold" of the day; gradually, if we keep moving, the warmth returns to us. It seems to me that no matter how warm our "coat" of relaxation is from the weekend or a smooth time in our life—no matter how determined we are to retain our serenity—the harsh winds find the weak spots in our warm fabrics. Unless we keep moving, we will feel the cold of the moment for many moments.

I truly am grateful that I can move. There are many who are not able to do so. Often I hear elderly people express humorous gratitude that they "woke up this morning." How absolutely true, even with no humor attached. My mother is greatly challenged, and often frustrated, because she cannot remember—not what happened an hour ago or what she is supposed to do two hours from now. Not knowing how to comfort her the other day, I told her how many people spend a fortune on books and classes just to be able to live in the moment. I explained that she should feel proud that she had accomplished this feat without any effort and had not spent a dime to achieve it. She laughed, of course, but it did make me think. We work so hard to live in the moment—to forget about what is done that cannot be undone and to stop worrying about what might happen tomorrow. The elderly and mentally impaired live that way naturally and yet we do not view this as an accomplishment. They challenge us because they are living in the moment. Our human limitations do not see it as the gift it is. It is hard for us to accept the very thing we are striving for.

May I more graciously accept the challenges of the elderly and impaired and live and love in the moment without imposing limits on what those gifts might mean. May I continue to move and be warmed by the motion of life even on the days when my heaviest coat does not keep out the cold.

SILLY

Rain came falling straight down, dripping from the massive trees and sending rivulets of muddy water flowing through the sodden grasses and soggy road. This is the time of suspended animation as the earth awaits the arrival of spring. Today is like many winter days but there is an expectancy that hangs upon the still air that makes the wet, barren day bearable.

I was recently advised not to make a decision "based on something silly." I thought about this advice for some time, wondering why it bothered me so much. I believe it is because everyone has their own definition of "silly" and something that might not seem significant to one person is incredibly significant to another. One of our greatest challenges as humans is that we seem compelled to want to impart our values onto others. While I applaud our confidence, we should temper our need to have everyone be just like us. One of our greatest advantages as humans is that we are all different with incredibly unique experiences that weave through us and create who we are and what we value. We should focus on celebrating that exquisite gift rather than feeling everyone should be the same.

I was surprised at how deeply the "silly" advice touched me. I realized it was a "lesser than" statement—statements we make all the time without really thinking about how our words might affect someone else. We all make choices in life that bring us the experiences that *we* chose; these are not the experiences others chose for us. If we allow others to make our choices and do not listen to who we are inside—that light that guides us so adeptly—then the joy of creating our life and learning from life is lost.

The light within is not necessarily logical or orderly but it is always correct if we listen and allow it to guide us without the chatter of our external world. Tuning out the chatter is the really difficult part, especially since we live in such an analytical space. To be still, to trust the inner voice, to seek the path the light shines upon is a lifetime quest of mine and there are days when I do not succeed. Those are the days when I am humbled by my own sadness or frustration. Those days serve as a reminder to go back to the listening so that I might find joy. Those days teach me not to push my values onto others but to have my own convictions and live my own life in the way that is aligned to who I am and what I want.

Today I wish to revel in the knowledge that we make our own choices and live according to our own unique joy. It is my hope that I will look back upon my life and have no regrets for the paths I have walked because I took the time to listen to the light within.

MASTERS OF FLOW

The sky was filled with individual puffs of clouds—connected, yet separate—like wool on a sheep's back. Were there patches of blue between the white, or were there patches of white upon the blue? There was a golden, glowing gap between the deep, dark blue of the distant hills and the coverlet of clouds as the sun rose on this winter's morning. The clouds took me away from the scrambling thoughts in my head and made me think about the lesson they might teach us here on the surface of the earth.

Clouds are masters at going with the flow. They are constantly changing and moving as the wind joins forces with the sun. They are unique, yet common. Sometimes they race but not to a destination. Their destination is ever changing. Sometimes they billow and glide across the sky. They can gather together as one or hover angrily over the land, dumping pelting raindrops on all around them. They can lilt along, catching sunlight or moonlight as they create magnificence in the air. But always, they are in motion. Serene or turbulent, they move.

Humans are also always in motion. We, too, are moving onward and though we believe we have a destination, like the clouds we only have a journey. We stand alone, but we are linked to the commonalities of mankind. There are times when we race across the sky of life, times we dump our anger on those around us, and moments when we allow our magnificence to seed our skies with rainbows and the flowing dances of the clouds. And we are always in motion.

What clouds have mastered is the acceptance of motion. We pull against it and the clouds just morph and flow because it is their natural way of existence. The motion in our life takes us to new places, new experiences, new stages. It carries us through sorrow, disappointment, love, and joy. Regardless of what we do in our human state, we cannot stop the motion. It is the natural way of existence. Finding the acceptance of moving and enjoying the ride on the wind is our challenge. We have greater impact on the quality of the clouds that skirt our skies than nature allows these visions of vapor, but we cannot control the forward movement of life.

The clouds in our life will not always be lilting, lingering, or reflective of beautiful light. The certainty is that we are always moving. This allows us to move through the darker, more turbulent times, knowing tomorrow will bring the softness and the peace again. This is the flow of life. It is the choices we have that make us different from nature. May we be wise in using the gift of choice.

FORGOTTEN TEMPLE

The wind was in its haven this morning, tossing the trees and huffing at the gray clouds that filled the sky. The barren branches in the orchard were stark against this gray backdrop. In the tallest tree, a group of eight robins were perched upon the limbs like Christmas ornaments. I noticed all around me the trees had tiny little points on their branches now, like miniature spears. Buds were starting to form, slowly. And only last night I heard the muted chorus of frogs that had emerged from their muddy blankets on a day that teased us with reminders of spring. But, indeed, though the days ahead may bring us stormy, cold weather, spring is laying the foundation for its splendor. Strong, calculated awakenings are stirring amongst nature. Nature is patient. I am not.

There is so much in life that we take for granted. We could chastise ourselves, but this is really an element of our humanness and, in some respects, protection from the bazillion thoughts we have on a daily basis that must be sorted in order to remain sane. However, on occasion, we should pay attention to the things that slide by us without acknowledgment or appreciation. One of those things is our health.

Our health is one of the most significant factors that

we forget to be grateful for. I have observed over the years the impact illness can have on our lives and the lives of those around us. The simple act of moving our fingers is completely unnoticed until we break one, cut one, or end up with a sliver. Suddenly we are amazed at all the things we can no longer do, or can no longer do easily. *Now* we appreciate our fingers. And they are only a tiny piece of what our bodies do for us. I have heard the human body described as a temple and yet we do not give it the reverence of a temple at all. A temple is a place of peace and prayer. We thank mystical powers in a temple. When was the last time you thanked your mystical toes or nose?

I am not a fitness freak or a health nut. In fact, I rather relate to the sloth, and pasta and frosting are a part of many of my favorite memories. I am not obsessive about health; I believe any time something controls you, you restrict the flow of life and miss the excitement of living. However, I also have a deep regard for the magnificence of good health. It really does not matter how much money you have, what you look like, what your title is, how perfect your children are, what house you live in or car you own—if you do not have your health, your world is very different. Suddenly, all which seemed so urgent is diminished to its rightful place. So much that mattered instantly does not.

Illness changes us. I have watched it change the people I love; I have watched it change people I don't even know. Sometimes there is an explanation for it, and sometimes there is no explanation at all. We can affect our health through our practices in life but even perfect practices do not guarantee our well-being. So I choose the middle road. I believe that joy and positive energy play a significant part in how we interact with our temple. Mostly I am grateful each day that all those fascinating elements of our physical structure work together, move together, make magic together, and allow me the freedom to "be" without limitation.

When you count your blessings, take a breath and say thank you that you can.

FLAMES OF LIFE

The fog was hanging on the trees today, obscuring the winter sun that promised to shine but had not yet awakened from beneath the misty blanket of morning. A deep chill in the air penetrated the warmest of coats and gloves and turned the feathery fog to cold fingers on warm cheeks. Fog brings with it a stillness, a sense of waiting for the air to move and release the earth from uncertain light. I was cold this morning, and upon returning from my walk, I built a fire.

I was mesmerized by the leaping, dancing flames of the fire. Though I know there is a scientific explanation for fire, it is really quite amazing if you think about it. It falls into that category of tangibly intangible. It is like golden air. While the fire warms the room, it warms the pockets of my soul even more. On stormy life days, a fire will soothe the inner tension and raise the level of contentment in my thoughts with graceful ease. The power of fire goes far beyond its physical warmth.

Fire, to me, represents our passions. When I speak of passion, I am not speaking of the things we like or enjoy but a deeper sense of purpose and mission that we carry within us and that drives us to take risks, make sacrifices, dance in our hearts, and sigh with satisfaction when we are fulfilling them. Like the fire, if we feed and fan our passions, they continue to leap, crackle, and spark. Sometimes we forget to nurture them and they slip lower to the ground and become tiny embers buried deep inside. On occasion, we even allow them to die completely. The fascinating thing about our passions is that, like the smoldering fire, a simple breath can bring them to life once again. They are the very fabric of who we are and they want to thrive within us. They are the very essence of the gifts we share with the world.

It is easy to let our passions become embers. We are so involved in everyday life that we forget to add a piece of wood to the blaze within. Sometimes we even forget to breathe our spirit into our life although every day we have opportunities to do so. I would encourage us all to touch the fire—the passion—we hold inside and allow the flames of our deepest hopes to dance and bring warmth to our world. Nurture your dreams and make them real. Breathe on the embers of what stirs you and feel the excitement in your soul. Let the spark of your passion ignite the fires of others, for they are drawn to the flames just as you are. Sharing our passions, moving with them and toward them, is what we are intended to do. Our passions inspire life.

Build a fire today. Turn on an electric fireplace. Light a candle. Watch the flame. And may the flame remind you to care for the passions that burn within you.

YIN AND YANG

As daylight was born, the sun began to penetrate through the fog. Heavy droplets of water clung to the barren branches and the needles of the conifers. The wand of a sunbeam turned them to prisms, shimmering like crystal beads. The day suggested it would be as beautiful as yesterday once the rays of the sun unfolded the shadows and the valleys from winter's hiding place. People came streaming from their housebound caves just to experience an hour of unexpected sublimity. In the Northwest, you never take sun for granted. Yet deny us the rain for too long and we yearn to feel it upon our faces.

I have a love/hate relationship with technology. It is as invasive as a blackberry bush and blossoms as brightly as a dandelion. I am alternately overcome with being powerful and powerless, feeling savvy in one moment and dense in the next. I am delighted to be able to write my words so easily, yet I want to hold a book in my hands. Technology makes me feel old in an instant—there is satisfaction in the fact that technology ages faster than we do—and yet I am bereft without it. I become frustrated faster with technology than I do with insurance companies. I love it when it works and I absolutely hate it when it doesn't. It holds us hostage at the same time it sets us free. Advances in healing, innovative solutions to challenges, and incredible convenience we now take for granted come with the price we pay. We have access to more information and people than ever before, yet we spin with the overstimulation of too much, too fast.

If you type quickly these days you are considered to be a good communicator. Studies show that our children today have serious deficits in interpersonal communication but thrive in the virtual communities. I am undecided on the role technology should have in our world today, but it is here to stay and the question is simply how much technology I will embrace in my life. How am I ever going to keep up without a microchip myself? If I just had a memory card this would be a lot easier!

I have more protected passwords than I can protect. I need index cards to keep track of when I'm me123 and when I'm 123me. Sometimes I'm wired, sometimes "-less"; sometimes I live in Google docs and the next minute I'm in spreadsheet workbook number three. I work with people in every time zone with every imaginable technological calendar. I have voicemail, e-mail, text mail, Skype, an iPod, Wii—who named these things anyway?—video chat (thank heavens I can control that one), Bluetooth, Facebook, instant messaging, instant internet, and a headache at the end of the day. I am at the beck and command of the world at any given moment. Interestingly enough, studies have shown that with our 24/7 availability we now work more than we ever did and accomplish less. Our primary interactions have become words while the scientists report only 7 percent of our capacity to communicate is through words alone. Of course, there are emoticons to help us. . . .

The flip side to all of this is that we have become a more global world. Our boundaries of communication are now limitless. We have conveniences and knowledge and relationships we could never have had without technology.

If I didn't feel quite so stupid most of the time, I would be awed! Truly, in its invasive way, technology is a step toward bringing us together as one world. It may be the catalyst that ultimately moves us toward greater understanding of humanity as a whole. This would be worth the pace and perplexity of technology.

All that said, I think it is very important for us to establish boundaries. We are addicted to our technology and we forget to nurture and cherish other parts of our lives that suffer from this attachment that moves us ever faster through our days. We need to establish rules and break the bond we have with technology for short periods of time so we can experience air, earth, and freedom. Computers operate on codes. They do not possess passion, love, or joy, where the very essence of the human spirit resides. We do not want to forget to nourish these unique elements of our existence.

Life is often about finding the balance between being still and moving forward. Balance comes when you take ownership of what is important in your life. Technology is an awesome tool if we remember that it is not life itself.

SPRING

PAUSE BUTTON

I tucked my gloved hands into the sleeves of my coat as I walked this morning. The air was chilled and a slight breeze made it even colder. The morning brought a respite from the deluge of rain and wind of yesterday and the sun even made a few brief appearances, peeking from holes in the dark clouds. I could see the path the water had taken on the gravel road. Fallen fir needles made little dams and barrier reefs, causing the path to twist and turn, slowing the potential devastation of too much water too soon.

The path of life is much like the path of the streaming water from a downpour. There are barriers and dams along the path—it doesn't run straight. Generally I think of barriers in a restrictive way; they impede the flow of life. But in looking at the water today, I had to wonder if they are meant to do so, or if they are the pause button for us so we do not run headlong to a destination that would be destructive without life's encouragement to be thoughtful. These barriers slow down the pace and provide us with some time to consider and ponder before we tumble along. I had never really considered the bumps in life to provide this purpose, but perhaps they do.

The challenge for us is to know when these bumps are barriers that provide us time to think and make good choices, and when we use them as excuses for not making progress in the stream of our life. Sometimes we only move on when the flow of life is so restricted that it spills over the dam, or breaks through the dam, in a gush and rush. Sometimes we simply wait until we seep into the ground so we don't have to move at all. How do we know when we are being given the gift of thoughtful restriction rather than fearfully holding back our potential and promise? Perhaps simple awareness of the difference is a first step—taking a breath and asking ourselves the question and being willing to hear the answer.

I am thinking today with a new perspective on those fir-needle barriers in my life and am grateful for them. They slow down the rush of life so there is not too much, too soon to carry us in directions we never intended to go.

FRIENDSHIPS

For several days the temperatures have teased us with warmer winds and nights. The bulbs have poked their heads through the cold ground as though they knew long ago the secret of the lengthening days when they were only vague dreams for humans. As the night deepened, I heard the sound of spring in the darkness. The frogs were croaking their throaty song from watery ponds turned warmer. What a beautiful sound!

We have many acquaintances in a lifetime, and lots of friends, but there are those rare individuals who are simply much more. They come into our life with a different connection, instant bonds of friendship and understanding, energy that is given to us rather than taken from us, and a safe space to be loved for ourselves. These individuals are very special gifts.

Friendships like this are not limited to humans. We have two cats who share this same bond and we can learn from their relationship, for they do not have to analyze and define life as humans do.

First, I must explain these two characters. Zeus is the king of cats. He is, without question, the alpha male of the house. He is a long, lean, feline machine who would absolutely fall into the category referenced in the quote: "If cats could talk, they wouldn't." Zeus is the picture of grace and dignity; he makes no wasted moves. He saunters down the outside stairs. When he hunts, it is not about catching, it is about killing—and we are talking rabbits and field mice the size of moles. Super is our other character. He loves everyone and everything and goes with the flow. He is never aggressive and seems to just shrug his shoulders when the other cats are aggressive to him. Super falls in the communication category of "Hi, I'm Super. Would you like to pet me?" He has very big feet and doesn't take the stairs—he plummets down the bank. His hunting capabilities follow the "catch and release" theory and are limited to little shrews, baby mice, and small birds. We have never figured out if he doesn't want to hurt other creatures or if he just doesn't know how to.

They make an unlikely pair of friends, and yet Zeus adores Super and Super worships Zeus. They are always together. Often you look outside and see only two sets of ears peeking up over some object, side by side. They sit on top of the stair railing like two sphinx, they peer off the deck sitting right next to each other, they sleep on the bed together, and they talk to and kiss each other. There is no aggression on the part of either. If Zeus feels Super needs a reminder about who is in charge, it is with a flick of the paw—no claws and no verbal reprimand. Any time you see one, you will see the other only a stone's toss away. You can almost see Super trying to mimic Zeus and he most often fails miserably. Zeus knows this but it doesn't matter to him. For some reason, Super has rights and privileges no other feline or human in this house has. Their friendship is pure, true, and heartwarming. They have been given this precious gift.

There are, on occasion, rare individuals who impact our lives in the most positive way. Sometimes they leave our life, sometimes they remain close beside us, but their love and acceptance of who we are is a priceless gift that remains with us always. They become part of who we are, and all that we will become. Whether in thought, prayer, or words, thank them today for touching your life.

RUBBER LIZARDS

Lilting music from birds everywhere greets the warming dawn. An unexpected surprise of the promise of sunshine and blue skies causes their chorus to grow ever more joyful with each trill. Hope is almost a tangible force when a day arrives so early in spring that reminds us how glorious a day can be. Soon there will be a flourish of fresh finery brushing across the land. It is the unexpected in life that transforms our viewpoints.

I don't think you can say you have truly lived until you step on a jelly rubber lizard in the middle of the night. There is no faster way to go from inner peace to profanity. This is a more common experience for young parents. For grandparents it serves as confirmation that you can move much quicker than you had believed possible! It is a lesson in agility, rude awakenings—hopefully you are not on your way to the bathroom—and absolute gratitude as it quickly dawns on you that what is beneath your feet is rubber and not real. Once your heart rate returns to a normal pace, you are also grateful for the little ones in your life who have successfully reminded you that living does not mean constant serenity. Sometimes there are a few rubber lizards just waiting to surprise you.

We often strive for perfection. We believe that if we

just achieve perfection in all aspects of our life, then, and only then, will we be happy. There is always one more thing to buy, one more thing to do, one more pound to lose (or twenty), one more week to work, one more obligation to fulfill . . . and *then* we will be happy and at peace. We are constantly striving to accomplish enough to find happiness rather than pausing to appreciate the happiness in everyday life. The trick is to capture the joy in imperfection—to appreciate what rubber lizards teach us. I have always been delighted that my husband is not perfect because then I do not have to be perfect either. If I had to choose, I would elect to have little handprints on my windows and toys to step on unexpectedly over a pristine and perfect existence any day. Without the surprises and bumps along the way, we are not really living; we are merely taking up mortal space.

The thing about rubber lizards (in the dark of the night or in life) is that they are rubber. They are not real. In that instant when they arrive in our life we think they are real but usually they turn out not to be. Often we spend so much energy on the rubber lizards that we forget to acknowledge all that is good and real in our lives. We miss the opportunities to experience the joy of life's imperfection.

May you recognize, and appreciate, one moment of unexpected, simple happiness today and laugh at the rubber lizard in the night.

QUIET BRILLIANCE

The tentative spring sunlight slipped through the clouds and sprinkled light upon the earth, which had been deprived of these golden ribbons for some time. At just the right angle, it brought to life vibrant green moss clinging to the barren trees in the deeper woods. Most of the year the brilliance of the moss is missed, lost amongst leaves or the gray of winter. Today it was bright and obvious and alive. Smattered here and there amongst it were ferns, thriving from whatever spirit within the tree nourished this unexpected life.

Not all the trees grow moss. I wondered why. I thought about people I knew, or had known, who also stood quietly and encouraged others to grow, content in sending others out to be the stars. The mossy trees, and these nurturing people, are firmly planted in the world, often lost among the vivaciousness of the taller firs and splendid foliage around them. Yet within them is some kind of magic—some kind of flowing life—that moves other creatures to cling to them as they grow. Without this simple stance and encouragement, others would never become what they could be.

In my life I have been blessed by just such people. Without the steady support of these people who believed in me, listened to me even when I made no sense, weathered my passions and my disappointments, touched me with a quiet word, helped me keep my feet on the ground, and picked me up when I fell, I would not know the joys or the accomplishments of today. The wings I fly upon belong to them, those quiet, nurturing souls who shape the lives of others and find deep satisfaction in doing so. I honor them, knowing the importance they play not only in my own life but in all the lives they are a part of.

So it is with deep gratitude that I acknowledge the powerful force of the supportive people in my life and give a nod to the mossy trees for the quiet gift of nurturing they bring to the world. Unexpected sunlight slipping across the land, thank you for reminding me.

ANTICIPATION

The birds are announcing spring. The human calendar has not yet made this transition, but nature does not live by the days on a calendar. Their songs are merry and many on these early March mornings. Today there was still that lingering winter chill in the air, with dark rain clouds hovering. From a distance, the heavy moisture glazed the fields and turned them opaque. On closer observation, each blade of grass, fence post, and tree branch was painted with individual raindrops. These clinging drops give a different perspective to what we simply label rain. The buds are swelling more every day on the trees and early flowers, with a soft shifting from brown to green as the earth peeks through the wafting fog and clouds. Only yesterday a hummingbird found the feeder I hung on the deck. The anticipation of spring is everywhere.

Anticipation. I read a statistic about anticipation the other day. It stated that we spend 40 percent of our time anticipating a coming event, 40 percent of our time remembering and relating the event, and only 20 percent of our time actually experiencing the event. Although I have no idea how the scientists arrived at these statistics, I do believe the basic premise of the numbers. Our species has a very hard time living in the moment. We think about the joy to come, we remember the joy we knew, and we forget to live the joy of now. How fascinating, and yet how sad. How much we miss by only experiencing the world around us and within us in the future or past tense.

This statistic caused me to pull myself into the moment today. As I walked, I noticed the iridescent raindrops on the leaves, heard the soft cooing of a mourning dove in the distance, looked up at the pussy willow paws emerging from the branches, and wiggled my fingers in the warmth of my gloves. I sat in my home office and felt grateful for the radiating heat from the funky fake fireplace, the glow of the lamp on my desk, the click of my fingers on the computer keys, the opportunity to feel fulfilled by accomplishing the tasks on my list. I glanced up, and there was a beautiful deer munching on the ivy on the bank right outside my window. I stopped and leaned back in my chair. I felt the warmth of the mug of tea on my hands, the contentment of living in the moment watching this graceful creature peacefully eating breakfast. A welcome break from the "urgency" of e-mail and conference calls.

I could not have anticipated this moment. It made me more aware of how much I had been living in anticipation of spring and not appreciating the magic that surrounds me with or without sunshine and daffodils. As it has long been said, "Tomorrow never comes." Let us find the joy in today.

KINDNESS MATTERS

The mist is hanging over the earth, billowing across the hilltops like smoke and clinging to the grass and trees. There is a subdued hush in the air. The birds are not singing gallantly like usual and the air has ceased to whisper in the ears of man. There is almost a tangible expectancy that the power of the sun will prevail and shift the momentum of the day to a brighter state.

The power of the sun is similar to other powers that are effortless and natural. In spite of the gray—whether in nature or life—deep and natural powers bring brightness and light to the world. I believe one of those powers is kindness. I often say, "Kindness matters." In fact, there is a sign that hangs by my front door inscribed with those words so all who live here and visit are reminded that kindness really does matter. I totally believe it does, but I asked myself the other day, "Why *does* it matter?"

Kindness offers a glimpse of the very best in people. In that moment of kindness, the window to heart and soul opens and faith in the goodness of humanity is restored for those who either give kindness or receive it.

If we equate who we truly are, and who we pretend to be, to that concept of a window, we will find that we spend a great deal of time sealing the window to keep the air out or in, covering the window up, and shutting ourselves inside. Sometimes in a burst of insight, we wash our window (or hire someone else to help us wash our window—called a psychologist), but in a short time we begin installing curtains and shades again. Occasionally we peer out of it but seldom throw it wide open with abandon to experience all that flows in and out. It is our filter. As we move through life, we shut our window more and more, fearing to venture out and show others our vulnerability. When we are kind to others, we are, in that moment, opening the window and sharing that vulnerability so that others might share theirs. In our vulnerability is our true and delightful self. A simple touch of kindness opens our window and, interestingly enough, this occurs whether we are initiating the kindness or are the *recipients* of kindness. Kindness allows us to experience the very best of ourselves and others.

Kindness is as powerful in our lives as the sun is to our earth. Remember that kindness matters. Because it does. Open the window and let your light shine.

SETTLED SILT

The wind had stopped breathing. In the stillness, the birds were filling the air with cheerful sonnets and acrobatics in the sky. Though clouds would not allow the sun to fall upon the land, there was a quiet peace and promise of change. Yellow was beginning to show on the daffodil buds, and the mud puddles and the water in the ditches were sleek like glass, revealing with absolute clarity each stone and leaf lying atop the silt that had settled to the very bottom of the watery wells.

Our lives are not dissimilar from the mud puddles and the ditches. When life is pelting us with driving raindrops and gusting winds, we find that our life is swirling with silt and muddy water that prevents us from seeing anything in our world with clarity. In the times when we are able to still the pace of life and step back for a moment from the turbulence and speed, the silt settles and clarity abounds. We see all the aspects that we often miss when churning challenges muddy the waters of life.

I think it is sometimes difficult for us to find the stillness. Yet if we do, we are compelled to find it again, for the clarity is a welcome sight and settles our souls, balancing us even as the battering rain and wind blows across our waters. We remember the vision and keep reaching for it in spite of the stirring of daily life.

As I turned on my computer, the rain began and the wind picked up. I knew that the perfectly still puddle that I experienced a moment ago in my thoughts would quickly shift back to the murkiness that the task of living often creates. But I also knew that at the end of the day, I would find a way to move myself back to the stillness—back to the place where I could clearly see each leaf and pebble nestled softly amongst the smooth silt of life. I now understood the value of allowing life to settle.

THE DAFFODIL PRINCIPLE

Today I saw the first trillium of spring, pure and white, and a stark contrast against the still-barren forest, emerging as though it were a scout for more blossoms to come. In pausing to admire its beauty, I was startled by a whooshing sound. Confused for a moment at the source of the sound, in an instant I realized it was the sound of the beating wings of a low-flying flock of geese.

Paying attention is one of the most important lessons in discovering the magic of everyday life. I admit to gazing out the window while sitting in a corporate meeting on the east coast last week. I was watching the birds (and listening of course), when suddenly the most brilliant red cardinal appeared. I was simply ecstatic. I had never seen a cardinal before and there it was, right there! It made the long trek across the country worthwhile, a little thing that speaks to us of hope and wonder.

Daffodils are my heroes. In January, they begin their trek up through the ground, peeking out cautiously and slowly rising in preparation for spring. When the cold winds roar, they simply stop in suspended animation and wait another week before moving upward again. They continue this pattern of plodding until they are standing tall and their yellow buds burst into the world with glory and promise of softer days to come.

Yet the spring is not so kind to these sturdy flowers. The winds toss them and the rains pour down upon them, adding a heavy burden of moisture to their stems and blossoms. The daffodils bend lower and lower but they are strong. Their bright countenance continues to grace the world around them even though the weight of the incessant rain pulls them to the muddy ground below. The skies clear and they lift up their faces to the sun, regardless of being battered and splattered by wearisome weather, and we smile because of their resilience.

I want to be like the daffodils. In spite of the obstacles that might fall upon my mortal path, I wish to be steady and strong, bringing to life the willingness to rise up and face the light, regardless of the disappointments and hardships that may forever change me. I hope the daffodils' positive presence on the rainiest days will always inspire me to do the same, bringing the hope and promise to my soul that these magnificent flowers bring to the earth. When life gets me down, may I remember the Daffodil Principle: steady myself, take a step upward, and offer a joyful countenance to the world around me.

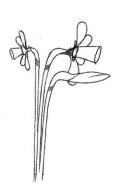

INSIDE LIGHTS

I feel very grateful today to have the opportunity to intimately watch spring appear on the hilltop during my morning walk. The first trilliums are emerging, and there are tiny leaves on the wild rose bushes. Other underbrush also sports newly extending leaves of green, turning the forest into a wellspring of hope and new life. Dots of white flowers here and there delicately poke their pristine faces to the sky. The daffodils are almost open and little dew-drop star flowers are swinging gracefully in the spring breezes. With every step I watch the miracle unfold, reminding me of the circle of life and filling my heart with promise and hope.

This evening, the clouds were dark, thunder echoed through the air, and the rain poured down upon the unfolding spring in torrents. My husband and I sat by the fire with our cats in warmth and contentment, watching the show outside our windows. We were safe and happy. In this moment, I thought about the peace we shared inside the shelter of our home. I also thought about how the outside of the houses we live in say nothing about the quality of life within these walls. There seems to be very little correlation between the exterior of a house and the sanctuary inside. We forget this sometimes, pining for the bigger, more beautiful, more luxurious house, although the house may not bring us the delight of a warm and loving home. We look at people the same way, pining for the beautiful, perfect exterior and forgetting that the light inside is unrelated to the shell.

The inner light is what you feel when you close your eyes and keep your mind from weaving tales. Inner light is transparent and brilliant, soft and glowing, an intangible warmth. You cannot hold it, you cannot touch it, yet it is powerful and strong and all-encompassing. It shines divinely regardless of the shelter in which it resides. The inner light is what we miss when people leave our world. We are often so distracted by the outer shell that we are blind to the beauty of the light that shines steadily inside. Not only do we fail to see it in others, but we fail to see it within ourselves. We search for answers in the outer trappings of life, rather than seeking it within. I want to see the light in the people I meet. I want to feel the light within myself so that I will recognize it in others more easily and more often. I want to have the ability to look beyond the shell to the quality of life within and to remember to see people for who they are on the inside.

Do not look in the mirror today with critical eyes. After years of conditioning, this is a very difficult task for us to do. But today, look in your heart at the beauty of your inner light. It is the magic you carry inside and it is the magic through which you experience life.

LUNAR LESSON

In a moment, the clouds will win, the wind chimes will sing, and rain will splatter across the greening landscape. Cascades of pink and white blossoms will flutter to the ground—springflakes, I like to call them. The daffodils stand sturdy amidst the changing weather even when pelted by raindrops and still-chilly winds. Early spring seems uncertain.

Yesterday the rain had been drowning the land, coming sideways in visible sheets of drenching water. The air was cold enough to snow but the pelting raindrops had not quite made the transition to delicate flakes. Wind had tossed the trees. They swayed dramatically like long-legged women doing intense yoga routines.

I sat on my couch, blanket tucked about me, fire glowing and warm, and I watched the darkness outside of my window. And then I saw it. A soft glow melting through the dark of the clouds: the moon. Like a beacon of hope, there was a heavenly breath in the fierceness of the sky. The moon did not show its face, but you could feel the light of its smile through the night.

I have grown to love the moon. Its constancy is reassuring, its beauty subtle and soft, and its message as true as can be that quiet faith in powers beyond our mortal comprehension continue to guide us. When the wind and the rain, the cold and the snow, leave us feeling desolate and dark, we must remember the constancy and the faith. This is much harder to remember during the wintery times in life and in nature. I am always grateful for these reminders from the moon and feel renewed hope and faith in the mystery of life when it graces our sky.

May you always remember, with the constancy of the moon, that if you have faith, the light in life will always shine through.

CLOUDBURSTS

The sun shines brilliantly over the land when suddenly, seemingly from nowhere, dark gray clouds block the rays and send downpours of rain onto the emerging green. The skies shift and a magnificent rainbow appears, then dissipates as a harsh wind sends the trees swaying dangerously in the wet, soggy ground. Then the wind stops and the birds sing gloriously; the sun bursts through and white puffy clouds dot the sky. This is the shifting weather of spring—ever changing, a new experience every few minutes. We enjoy the moods of spring as though it were a mystery novel, never knowing what the next paragraph might bring.

In the big scheme of things, life is like this as well, new chapters constantly unfolding. In the day-to-day lives of humans, our emotions are like the spring weather. In any given twenty-four-hour period, we move on the emotional continuum even more often than the spring weather. We can feel ecstasy and peace one moment, and plummet to the darkness in an instant. We recover, move up through the pyramid, and then crash to the bottom again. Over and over and over. It seems a continuous quest to balance ourselves on a daily basis. It is something we do without any conscious thought, really. It is part of the human experience.

How lucky we are to be able to experience the changing

weather of spring. How lucky we are to experience life's changing weather as well. How boring we would be if we were not capable of the highs and lows of living. There would be no song to the wind without obstacles in its path. In my profession I have been taught how not to respond—how to keep constant control and clear thinking. And that's perfectly fine for that purpose. But at one point, I found myself carrying this mindset into my personal life, and that is not okay. We are born to experience life, not to flatline life. This does not mean we should continually engage in drama and trauma, for that is born from a very negative viewpoint. I absolutely believe that a positive approach to living creates a more positive and enjoyable life. Yet giving up some control, appreciating the ever-changing experience of being human and accepting this change with patience and humor, is essential to finding more moments of sunshine and rainbows, and fewer moments of angry clouds and downpours.

Will I ever achieve such spiritual depth that I live in joy every moment of every day? Perhaps when I leave this earth. But, I am quite convinced, not before that. I will, however, revel in the sunbursts and learn from the cloudbursts. Someone once said, "You can't have a rainbow without any rain." I'll live with the extremes to experience just one delightful, magical, magnificent rainbow each day.

NAPS

Slowly, ever so subtle and ever so silent, the dawn moves across the horizon. In mere seconds the hues of morning shift and change amongst the clouds that hang heavy on this spring day. Nuances and defining lines meld into one with the promise of newness to come.

Each morning there are forty-five minutes that are mine. While I'm not a morning person, these minutes have become my very favorite time of day. Dawn is quiet. Serenity whispers. Love and hope brush my soul. I cherish these moments so much that even on the days when I must leave before dawn to catch a plane, I weave into my beginnings some moments to absorb this beautiful essence of living, where silence is queen. Every day, I begin my day with this extraordinary pause.

A gray and rainy day. Mundane. Not quite spring and not quite winter. A very rare, very special day. How bizarre for me to say this about a random Saturday in March. The day that stretched before me contained no obligation. There was not one thing in it that had the possibility of letting someone down or holding them back if I did not do it—no task that would impact anyone or anything if I did not do it today. The cats and my husband might protest if I did not see to it to feed them, but that is minor in the scope of what my days are generally like.

What would I do or not do? I decided I would take a nap in the afternoon, listening to the rain outside and the crackle of a fire inside. Taking a nap is an absolute rarity for me and a total luxury. There has never been a time when I have not been engulfed in bliss while taking a nap. To simply slip away into dreamland where all things are sweet and peaceful, waking slowly and stretching easily like a feline, prolonging the divine before returning to the world—heavenly!

I thought about how unique this day was for me and how wonderfully freeing and indulgent it felt. I am quite certain I am not alone in finding few days to be without obligation. In spite of having a list of things to do today, I knew if I chose not to do them, no one would suffer. What a terrific gift! It served to emphasize how we fill our lives up with busyness and expectations. I am one of the greatest offenders of constantly having to accomplish something, be productive, and satisfy the needs of everyone around me. In my work, and in my home life, I try to do far more than is humanly possible in a day. The "achieve and succeed" motto is deeply ingrained in me and it is difficult to take a day like this one and let that all go. But the bliss of the choice to do so is absolutely exquisite.

What I have learned in living, and what I hope to practice, is letting go of my self-imposed need to do all things and be all things to all people. Live more easily, laugh more often, care less about things that don't really matter, accept me as much as I accept others, feel the flow of life slide through me as it will, and enjoy every moment that it does—even as I write these words, I realize I have a desire to "achieve" this.

Some things may never change. For now, I'm taking that nap!

BREEZES

With the first step today I knew my trek would be easier. The temperature was much warmer, the earth was sighing quietly, and the only breeze was the one I made myself with my forward motion. I could smell the earth and breathe in the softness and hope of gentler days ahead.

I am often amazed at the things we miss in life that suddenly become so clear. Just the fact that I was making my own breeze was surprising. We are always moving forward and making our own breeze in life. Our own breeze is gentle and kind, unrushed and without tension. Soft, sure, content. It is the outside forces—the external winds—that interrupt the sweetness of our own forward motion. Our own breeze is always with us but we often cannot feel it for the distractions of harsher, urgent, noisier currents.

When the wind around me is blowing, I am caught up in the sounds it makes, the impact it has on my body, whether cold or hot or angry or happy. My mind absorbs the turbulence, the excitement, the busyness of the world's wind. These winds around us are simply everyday events that are part of our daily routines and the tasks of living. Sometimes we encounter negative, dark winds that drain us of our energy. Sometimes we encounter whirling, twirling winds that are filled with excitement and knowledge. All are external forces that create our days and our emotions. But always there is the gentle breeze that leads us through life, though we often forget we are capable of making our own motion.

How do we keep the external winds in balance with the kinder, more content breezes of our inner selves? I'm not positive I have the answer. Perhaps awareness that the softness exists within us, and a conscious decision to find time every day to let that sweetness absorb us, will provide the perspective we need to experience contentment amidst the external winds that so often shape our lives and diminish our most important dreams. Let the forward motion of life be grounded in the breezes you make yourself.

DO-OVERS

I slipped out the door this morning to replenish the peanuts for the squirrels. It was still dark, with only a promise of dawn to come. But the birds, still nestled in the surrounding trees, were whispering to the world as though encouraging the sun to wake from its slumber. A quiet song. Later, as my steps carried me across the hilltop engulfed in the golden sunshine of a chilly spring morning, the birds were in full chorus, trills, whistles, and sonnets abounding across the land. The yellow violets were everywhere, joined by the pale lavender ground cover; leaves were emerging, small but sure, throughout the woods. For just a moment, I caught a waft of sweetness in the air reminding me that the world was in the process of being reborn.

How many times are we reborn in our lifetime? In many respects, I believe we are reborn each and every day. Each day brings us new possibilities and new adventures. Each night we put our day to rest, and each morning we awake into newness. Every new day we have the opportunity to start over. This is not the same as "do-overs"—we don't get those very often. What is done, is done, and cannot be undone, to paraphrase Shakespeare. But we certainly have the gift of learning and applying our lesson so that the next encounter will be better than the last. This is the evolution of the human spirit as we move through our lifetime. The human species has the ability to change and grow with life in a wondrous way. And as we move toward the end of our life, we simply outgrow this limiting mortal existence.

The trees inspired this thought. I noticed the height of the fir trees. They stretch up and touch the sky, their trunks solid and secure. As trees grow older, they become larger and stronger. As humans grow older, we become smaller and fragile. The trees outlive us by so many years if left untouched by man or the perils of nature. Through our years, our hearts and souls expand beyond our physical body's capacity to hold them, and so we abandon this limitation in search of a more expansive dimension where we can thrive and flourish more freely. The infinity we have been given is a beautiful thing, really; too difficult for those of us left behind to comprehend.

GIFTS

Pink trees as fluffy and full as clouds dot the awakening land. Hope is captured in a blossom. On windy days the blossoms cascade upon us, scattering their petals like fairies sent to remind the grass to grow, the leaves to unfold, the birds to sing. A fantastic gift for winter-weary humans.

I find gifts truly fascinating. The gifts I refer to are mostly intangible, given to us by powers greater than ourselves: gifts of time, relationships, jobs, children, financial gains, health, safety, and countless moments or happenings that fill us with happiness and gratitude. And on occasion, we receive gifts that we do not recognize as such until the time to be grateful has long passed.

With each gift we are given an opportunity to learn something about ourselves or about others. If you think about it, every gift you have been given has resulted in some kind of spiritual growth. So while we are regaling in the magnitude and appreciation of the gift, we are also about to enter a time when we might be challenged to observe something of great significance that has little to do with the actual gift and everything to do with why we received it in the first place.

The thing about gifts is that we must learn how to receive them. The human species has worked hard at learning how to give. We are taught early on how important it is to give to others. There is a great Reba McEntire song with the line, "If there's just one secret to living . . . it's learning the meaning of giving with an open heart." Indeed, it is. We strive for this. Yet I think we should also learn how to receive with an open heart—to say thank you, express our appreciation and gratitude, and feel it all the way through ourselves. It is okay to receive, as giving and receiving are a natural circle of life. Without experiencing each, we prevent the circle from moving and flowing in balance. I find in myself, and in others, that it is far more difficult to receive than to give. I need to work on graciously accepting the gifts that are given to me. I need to just say "thank you".

LIFELINE

'Tis the season of rainbows! Rainbows only grace our world when moisture and sunlight join, creating a breathtaking bridge between the two extremes. Often, only the beginning and the end of the shimmering bow can be seen, and we rely on our faith to know the two are connected. Life can be much the same.

It sometimes seems insensitive to write of joy and peace during times when there are great tragedies—times when others are feeling great losses and devastation. It is like trying to capture the magic and love of Christmas when your heart is broken. It feels more empty than full. I wish to acknowledge the pain that life sometimes brings to us.

There have been extremely difficult times and circumstances in my own life, though I seldom share this with most people. I think many of us are this way. Pockets of sorrow seem beyond words. When we talk of faith, it often seems like those who appear not to really need faith have faith easily, while faith is beyond the grasp of those who seem to need it most. I know that to even see joy or beauty in life seems like an impossible task when the inner and outer tears are so thick that sight is a daily struggle. I know that to experience a hollow echo in your soul can be so intense that any kind of positive vibration seems to be lost in the caverns of trepidation. I believe it is important to honor the losses, to feel the sorrows, and to grieve for the people and the things that we cannot reach or understand and are lost to us. I also believe that these are the times when we must ground ourselves in faith rather than thought.

As I was writing these thoughts today, it occurred to me that I have been feeling guilty for finding joy in my life when others I know are suffering so much. Guilt always tugs us downward rather than lifting us up. I realized that I needed to shift my perspective from guilt to gratitude for all the things I take for granted each day, knowing that in an instant life could change dramatically, and I could lose all the little pleasures and conveniences, all the people and security I experience every day but seldom even consider. Moving my focus to appreciation for what I have and sending heartfelt thoughts to those who had less was a much more positive and healing approach than allowing guilt to surround me for things over which I had absolutely no power to change.

We all experience devastating times in our lives. I am always in deep awe of those who overcome staggering odds to find a peaceful place in living beyond the moment when life fell out beneath them. I believe we can make two significant misjudgments in times when our spiritual feet fail us. One is to not acknowledge the pain and the loss—to bury it, deny it, or ignore it. The second is to live there forever more.

The capacity to love so deeply that we grieve so deeply is a gift for the human spirit. The fabric of our life becomes priceless beyond what we ever imagined. We are reminded of fragility and uncertainty, which humble and hold us. May these also remind us to fly, for we have felt and lived and known the love from which all joy and all sorrow is born.

NO RUNNING

The sun filled the sky today as dawn made its debut. Shadows that do not appear on the gray days fell across the earth. They shift and move, ever changing. Shadows are fascinating. They do not exist without sunlight and obstacles. They cast darkness but create a greater array of movement than the dull days of gray with no contrast.

This morning our youngest cat was racing through the house with abandon. It reminded me of our little grandsons who like to do the same, which is always followed by an immediate reprimand from an adult: "No running in the house!" As adults who are responsible for children, we do that alot. How often do we as parents say, "No running"? And yet if you think about it, as adults we run all the time. Our pace is often at that high speed. The difference is that usually our race is internal and many times it is not done with energy and enthusiasm. In fact, quite the opposite. It is usually tiring and often draining.

We tell our children to "stop running" because we know it is only a matter of time before they trip or run into an obstacle that will hurt them. It is our protective nature—our caution and concern for their well-being—that makes us tell them to slow down. Hmmm. Who tells *us* to slow down? We are bound, in our fast pace, to trip when our speed propels us to do something without thinking—sometimes even in the form of words we regret—or we end up in a situation where there is a barrier or obstacle that harms us or someone else. All because we forget to take our own advice to stop running.

I am as guilty of running through life as anyone. I must make a conscious effort to slow my pace to preserve my perspective, my balance, my thoughtfulness, my quality of living. Breathe. Exhale. These are words I use frequently to remind myself to walk—not run. Our youngest grandson responded to our "don't run" pleas in a great way. He walked slowly by his mom and then rounded the Invisibility Corner and ran through the room she could not see. Well, he eliminated half the risk! I think my practice of slowing my pace mirrors his. At least I gather some protection against the harm of "running" half the time.

May I remind myself to walk just a few times today so that when I need to run, my stride is grounded and steady. May I slow the pace so I do not trip so easily. Tripping is much too humbling.

GROCERY LISTS

As I went about my daily morning routine, I glanced out the window. Across the valley a ribbon of golden sunshine topped the trees and hills in the west, a band of light gracing the land. It was stunning! As I walked my morning path, I glanced down and saw that the winds of the previous days had tossed the small cones from the huge sequoia trees upon the road. These cones are very special. They have long, curving tails—"stems" in scientific talk—and I feel compelled to pick them up whenever I see them. I stashed as many of them as my pockets would hold and continued on my way. It is amazing how many things are truly phenomenal that we simply don't see as we make our way through life. Many days I do not see these things either but on the days when they come fully into my view, I am always awed by their beautiful presence.

Today I spent my weekly time in the grocery store. A fascinating place, if you think about it. I remember several years ago it was rumored that grocery stores would cease to exist—that everyone would purchase their food online. Now, we have accepted purchasing just about everything else online and we totally embrace this concept. But not our food. How funny we are! We mutter about having to go to the grocery store, we splutter about the prices, but we keep going. Why is that?

I observed the buzz and hum of the grocery store today. People pushing their carts about, debating what they would or would not purchase; the little ones hopping about and asking questions and getting in the way of the carts; the flow of cart traffic up and down the aisles; the older generation moving more slowly and buying much less; the displays of vegetables and fruits; the bakery smells; the ladies handing out samples . . . Grocery stores are the melting pot of neighborhoods, with rules and etiquette all their own. They are so much a part of our lives, and a part we have not allowed to change all that much.

The older my mother has become, the more important it is from her perspective to go to the grocery store. Shopping is a purpose, a routine, an opportunity to be around other people, even if they are strangers. The elderly—a group of people who would benefit most from having groceries delivered to their home—crave the experience of the grocery store. They know the checkers and where everything is. They seem to derive a sense of belonging and acceptance from the routine of grocery shopping. Life here is "normal."

In a world with less community and more self-sufficiency, I wonder if the grocery store does not in some bizarre way satisfy the basic human need for camaraderie. In a world that moves so rapidly and changes so much, perhaps the constancy of the grocery shopping experience provides a balancing point that we can count on and are unwilling to change. So much of our world spins with things over which we have no choice or control; maybe we really like the fact that we can at least choose what food we buy.

I went about my shopping, happily pushing the cart with the errant wheel, and admiring the array of coffee, cat food, cakes, and condiments. I felt satisfied with the treasures I would bring home, delight at the elderly men pushing the cart or carrying their wife's purse, and the busyness of everyone around me. Then, like a shock to my euphoria, I paid the bill.

THE NAVIGATOR

The earth was calling me to walk upon the land this morning. After days of rain and clouds, the sky was clear as the dawn began to move to daylight. A slight easterly breeze brushed my cheeks with a cold hand but the air felt good. Though the sun was still hiding below the horizon, it touched the white streams from the jets streams and turned them to glowing gold as they streaked across the sky like shooting stars. The streams were far more beautiful from where I stood than when I'm up there flying in them.

I was sitting in the small Vermont airport trying not to cry with disappointment. I had changed my flight to an earlier departure due to an impending snowstorm, but my flight was delayed to the point that, while I may miss the snowstorm, I was also going to miss my connecting flight in Chicago. I would spend a short night in a Chicago hotel rather than in my own bed with fleece sheets, kitties, and my husband. After a long week away from home, this was not what I had hoped for.

This was a defining moment. In my weariness, I realized what great lengths the universal power I so believe in had gone to in order to keep me from flying home this night. Oddly enough, I found myself saying, "Thank you for your extra efforts, I appreciate it." I had no idea why I was traveling—or not traveling—this path, but I was absolutely certain there was a distinct reason for it. Instead of being consumed by angst, I found a genuine feeling of gratitude.

Many times in my life I have experienced a redirected path, regardless of what I'd planned that path to be. Some of these are small, like sitting in a traffic jam and shifting my thoughts to being grateful I am sitting still rather than being crunched somewhere up ahead. Some of the shifts are deep and significant, like job changes or discouragements, health issues, family issues, or other obstacles of the heart. In all of this, however, I have learned that those "recalculations" (as my GPS likes to call it) have led me to exactly where I needed to be next, and almost always to a better place than I had imagined I would be. As impatient as I am, I have come to understand that the flow of my life is as it should be and I try to just step back and be grateful that there is a navigator far wiser and more knowing than I.

Each time the pattern shifts in my life, I learn something new. The term "lifelong learners" is not just for academics. It applies to all of our lives. There would be no joy, no excitement, no fascination in life if we were not in that learning state. I believe we are given the circumstances in which we might grow. What we do with those circumstances is how we learn. Some days I'm at a remedial level and acutely aware of it, some days I'm smart as a whip and sing with the joy of it, and some days I have no idea what the lesson might have been. But always I am grateful for the opportunity to have an outstanding human experience.

MOON MOMENTS

As I was entering the fast pace of the freeway this morning, I glanced upward to find a bright crescent moon rising in the east above the mountain that was just beginning to feel the golden rays of the sun. It was fascinating just to think about the fact that the sun and the moon were both rising in the east at the same time. At first, the glowing crescent of the moon was all I noticed, but in my second glance, I could also see the shadow of the entire moon, even though it was not lit.

Faith is believing in what you cannot see. The moon is such a good lesson for us. The crescent moon is like the focus of our life. It is illuminated with light because it is present and in our line of sight. We move through our life sometimes with this singular view, forgetting how much more exists. The shadow of the entire moon slips from our perspective—the shadow of all we cannot see in the moment or, perhaps more accurately, all that we fail to remember to see in the moment simply does not exist. It creates a limiting view of life and all that moves within it. Without the full circle of life being ever present in our lives, we focus on things that really don't matter as much as we think they do.

The sun is brilliant and captures the attention of everything and everyone with its glitz and power. The moon is dark without the reflection of the sun. Yet it seems perfectly content to thrive in this reflection and steadily, rhythmically, rises each day with total reliability and consistency. It is comforting and mystical. Its soft light falls easily upon the earth and only occasionally do we see it in its glory. Then it steps back and quietly goes on its steady path.

Not all of us can be the sun, the focal point, the power, the brilliance, the leaders. Many of us are the moon, quietly going about our way with a calm, steady, seemingly mundane routine. Yet I believe we are as essential and romantic as the moon. We set the pace. We shine, we step back, and we shine again, reflecting a light that is soft and beautiful and dependable. It is our motion that becomes the rhythm of life. The roles we play are equally as important to the balance of our world. Contentment then comes from being at peace with who we are and the roles we play.

ROUND SKIES

The sky was incredibly blue as I walked this morning. I thought about the sky and I began to visualize it as being round like the earth. Suddenly, I was seeing this familiar landscape in a different way, as though really seeing it for the first time. Walking on my flat, straight path, I could feel the earth "round." I can understand how in times past we thought the earth was flat. We seem to live life with sharp edges and flat planes. We seldom approach life with rounded edges. We are such an analytical species. It seems we need scientific explanations or logic for almost everything. Technology only deepens this tendency to analyze and record. If it cannot be explained in charts, graphs, and data, then it doesn't exist or is invalid. This is a battle I have fought all of my life. I give great credence to intuitive emotion. In our world, I am forced to put this "knowing" into analytical terms.

As a human resource professional, I interview and hire many people. Our analytical business world continually wants tools and measures to make hiring decisions, believing this is the way to select the right person for the job. Chance and instinct are taken out of the equation. They want to find a way to measure the intangible. I would agree that there are certain aspects of this process that help us hire talented and dedicated people. Yet I have found over and over again that intangibles are felt rather than measured. If someone goes against their gut, there is generally a very good reason for it, which all the statistics in the world won't reveal. I am continually balancing the analytical and the intuitive. Many books make an effort to teach us that our vision is flat, and that without seeing beyond this even plane and viewing the roundness of our existence, forward motion will never be the triumph we believe it should be.

The most powerful forces in our world cannot be measured or defined. Love is the perfect example. It just happens. It is a soulful connection that defies all logic and analytics. Take the current trend of online matchmaking. Logic lines up the pairing of interests, personality profiles, age, location, whatever. It all looks great and the two people chat online and then they meet. What is the explanation for the times when it truly does click and the times when it goes all wrong? Computers and technology and logic cannot predict with much accuracy the romantic chemistry of humans. If this powerful force cannot be explained, does that mean it does not exist? We possess powers that simply *are*. And, they are *round*.

I don't believe that life was intended to be sharp. The times when I have been absolute, viewing life from a flat perspective, I have fallen sharply off the edge. It hurts! I have grown to understand, and prefer, the wonderful roundness of evolving into tomorrow. When I was seventeen, I wrote, "Certainty is such a fleeting thing." I should have listened to that young self and saved myself the pain of believing today's answers would be tomorrow's as well—that my perspective was the only truth, and that the more knowledge I had, the wiser I would be. It is a challenge in our human world to remind ourselves that the earth, and life, is round. Flat perspectives and sharp edges are counterintuitive to the very nature of triumph.

TALL TREES

A southwest wind huffed through the trees as I walked this morning. The gravel road was quieter and calmer from a few days of rain. Brown fronds from the tall sequoia trees lay strewn across the road and around their trunks. The earth was better served by what had once been an essential part of the tree. The wind had gently removed the old so that the new might thrive. What is the equivalent of the gentle wind in our lives that helps us ease into the new and let the old slip sweetly away?

I find we are not so good at letting things slip sweetly away. We try to cling to what no longer serves us, and the parting, when we are forced to let go, is often more harsh than gentle. A constant motion moves us through ever-changing life. Change is as much a part of living as breathing. How we embrace this motion is up to us. As much as I strive to allow learning and letting go be a part of the motion of my life, I am acutely aware that I find this very difficult.

We are such complex beings. The intensity of the motion in our lives is pretty incredible. How we process the motion throughout a lifetime is even more incredible. Change allows us to let go of the old to make room for the new, for we simply cannot hold that much "stuff" within ourselves and maintain any kind of sanity. Being all things to all people all the time until death do us part is just not possible. Nor does it allow for the new to grow within us and around us and through us. We must learn to bless what is our past and let it fly away in the wind to a destination where new life will spring forth. No matter how comfortable we are wearing the past, it may not fit the occasion of today or tomorrow. But it is so hard to throw away that comfortable sweatshirt with the holes in it if we do not have absolute faith that the new one will be equally as soft.

If I can hold on to the lessons learned, the good I find in the memory, and allow the gentle winds to peacefully blow the rest to another place, then I will have accomplished much in this lifetime.

THE PRICE OF EGGS

The sun burst upon the spring landscape, scattering brilliant rays of light across the new life. The songbirds filled the air with the harmony and joy of a new day. Throughout the forest were the growing buds of leaves about to be born, flowers turned their faces to the sunlight, and the rabbits were hip-hopping everywhere. It was a glorious day, filled with promise and happy perspectives.

Perspectives are rather elusive. We often say we have to "regain our perspective" yet we always have a perspective—it's just at times rather dreary and delusional! Perspective is so unique to each of us and comes from . . . where? Sometimes it comes from the years' worth of messages we receive in life. A perfect example lies in the coloring of Easter eggs. How many times have I heard people lament that they don't know what to do with all those eggs. It's really quite simple from my perspective: throw them away! Who ever said you had to eat them? They're just fun! When was the last time you had fun for $3.00? I think it's pretty cheap entertainment. Yet years of conditioning have given us the perspective that we must eat the eggs. How many other perspectives are equally as bizarre?

I have always been inherently decisive, but I have learned that many times I must step back from that ability—

or disability—and look at life from a different angle. A different perspective. What is it that I don't know or cannot see from where I am? Perspectives can be limiting; by shifting our view, we can access thoughts and ideas we never knew existed. In my profession, it is imperative that I see situations from a different perspective. It is also imperative that I do this from my heart. Regardless of the chattering of my mind, my heart rules the decisions I make and so it is extremely important that I consider a different view before I leap into action, or reaction.

To put a slight twist on a great saying, if you always think what you always thought, you will always get what you always got. There is much in my life that I "got" that I love, but if there is something in my life I'm not happy to get, then I need to find a way to change my "thought" to find a new place—a new perspective—that will bring me closer to joy.

CARPODS

No perfume or candle can capture the real smell of spring. A subtle sweetness slips all around us, a freshness in the air that moves us to move again. A gentle, misting rain was falling this morning on the hilltop, nurturing the leaves and flowers just enough to thrive. A few days of warm sunshine had just passed. The ever-changing weather we mutter about is the exact measure of light and water, warmth and cold, that nature requires to allow hope to blossom about us. As humans, we have a much harder time finding that balance to blossom fully.

As I was driving (slowly) in rush-hour traffic one day last week, I looked at the cars creeping along all around me. And, as I frequently do, I began to ponder. Each vehicle was like a little "carpod." For in each carpod was a life teeming with activity, families, and emotion—concern, joy, love, anger, sorrow, anticipation, and regret. Each carpod was traveling to a destination, its driver consumed with where they were going, where they had been, health, children, spouses, parents, work, and all the other things that fly through our minds at any given moment. Each carpod represented a unique, individual life just like my own. Yet here we were, thinking we were so special unto ourselves, and we were all sitting in our carpods moving along. Seen from a higher altitude, we would appear to be one flowing stream of existence. It was almost overwhelming to consider.

In Miguel Ruiz's book, *The Four Agreements*, one of the agreements is "Don't take anything personally." As I sat in my car thinking about all these carpods around me and about a particular discussion that had left me distressed, I considered that statement. To truly live in a peaceful, spiritual place, we should achieve the Four Agreements, yet most of us do take things personally. The things that happen in our life, whether we are all really one or not, feel personal to us and it is very hard to put the pain aside when it impacts us deeply. So I simply acknowledged in this moment that my feelings were hurt; that I *was* taking it personally and I really did not know how to *not* do that. But it also gave me insight into the world of humans: all these carpods were also taking things personally and reacting as best they could. Some better than others, obviously!

Here in this space we occupy, we operate as solitary beings and take things personally because it feels very unique to *us*, regardless of what we intellectually know. That we are feeling, sensitive, flowing souls is part of what makes us so splendid. Very few of us are able to rise to a spiritual level where we do not take things personally. Yes, we need to step back from the drama we create for ourselves, but at the same time, we need to understand that it is part of our wondrous human nature to take things personally. And in this, we are not unique.

It goes back to that ever-present theme of balance— of cultivating a soulful approach to life where we keep our perspective and do not take things so personally and simply accept ourselves as imperfect but wonderful beings. It is the balance of deeply knowing we are all one and embracing our uniqueness at the same time. Each day we achieve this balance, we should celebrate with abandon.

EARTH STARS

Brilliant sunlight is embracing the young life of spring today. A pleasant morning with a promise of warm sweetness. Two bright yellow finches danced across the road on this glorious morning, and two rabbits skipped into the underbrush as I passed. Two seems to be the common theme for nature's creatures this time of year.

This was a travel week and as the plane descended into Chicago, I looked out at the flat, muted landscape. It was an ordinary view, just like most cities one flies into. However, every once in a while there was a sparkling flash of light—like twinkling earth stars—from ordinary objects that caught the reflection of the sun, turning into exquisite bursts for just a moment.

Returning to my regular, routine life today felt good and I walked upon my familiar earth reveling in that comfortable pace of solitude, not expecting any grand moment to arrive. Yet there it was, a turquoise-blue robin's egg alongside the path, almost out of place in the earthy turf. It was really quite exquisite. I thought about this anomaly in the world of eggs. Most eggs are bland in color—gray, white, cream, tan—a design by nature to make the eggs inconspicuous to predators who might find them tasty. Yet here was this robin's egg, as outstanding and lovely as could be. I wonder why, in the grand scheme of things, the non-descript robin was chosen for such a bright and cheerful egg.

We spend most of our living moments in the land of the ordinary. There is a certain security in this that sets the stage for those other moments—the exquisite ones—to stop us in our tracks, catching our breath at the beauty captured there. These moments are not just about beautiful things, but about awesome emotions that slip into our life on rare occasions. Though they make up far less of our living days, they inspire and sustain us. We remember them and count on them and thrive upon them. These awesome moments lift us up and we find ourselves unexpectedly reflecting light, just like the muted objects in the Chicago landscape, turning from mundane to magnificent.

Robins are a pretty ordinary, common bird but they bring us positive promise in their exquisite blue eggs. I believe we all have unexpected blue eggs to share with the world.

CEILING FANS AND UNDERWEAR

Unusually warm weather drifts across the emerging green of the landscape. Honeybees are already busy spreading life amongst the blossoming trees that fill the air with a sweetness only spring can provide. The breezes are subtle and leave the earth craving a slightly cooler day. Humans are also unaccustomed to the warmth, and ceiling fans that have been dormant for the long winter months begin to hum. Most of us revel in the cool air, but there are some who can see far beyond the functionality of a fan.

Our daughter strongly encourages her young children to keep moving along the routines of morning so she can get them out of the house and on the road on time. One day, her two young boys were given explicit instructions to get dressed while she was doing the same. Suddenly she heard raucous laughter and squeals from the kitchen. With boys, one must be compelled to go check when this occurs. As she stepped into the kitchen, my daughter was greeted by her sons' pajamas and underwear spinning around on the ceiling fan with two triumphant, nearly naked youngsters laughing with total and absolute delight. They had succeeded in putting a new "spin" on an old routine.

Laughter and delight. If we could all start every day like this, the world would no doubt be a much better place. If we could see the joy and fascination in our common, functional, everyday routines, we would all be smiling more and frowning less. No wonder children bring us wonder! They are amazing at dancing when there is no music and laughing when we have forgotten how.

I found our grandsons' early-morning experiment absolutely inspiring. No, I did not throw my underwear on the ceiling fan, but I sure laughed a lot. The Pajama Challenge compelled me to look for the lighter side of living and to remember how much better life can be when we take ourselves a little less seriously and find ways to brighten even the most common of days.

Perhaps today would be a good day to not only look for unexpected delight but to create it.

VALUE TO THE DAY

Sunlight was pouring through the forest, glinting, glowing, sparkling, leading the dance. Such power! Such warmth! Such an inspiring display of energy for all creatures on this earth that are irresistibly drawn to the bright light.

I had the opportunity to work with a gentleman a few years ago who possessed such an optimistic, warm, engaging personality that people were drawn to him immediately. Any time you needed a smile he would be there with one just for you. His smile was not a façade. It was genuine. Each month we presented together at new employee orientation and though we had memorized the script of each other's presentation, each time he presented I gave great thought to the quote he used: "It is not about being paid by the hour but about the value I bring to the hour." It is such an awesome quote used by an awesome man. He did bring value to each day—each hour—and though we worked hard to achieve our goals, we also had fun doing so. We were totally in sync and we found great joy in working together and for the mission of the company.

So often I speak of personal life rather than business life, though the business world has certainly taken up much of my personal time over the years. Many of us would say that "work is work" and "home is home." I would agree to a point.

I am actually quite passionate about my work and about the companies I work for. However, I am also passionate about finding balance and seeking a "whole" life that is fulfilling and, well, soulful. There truly is joy in a job well done, in a team that works together without ego to reach a common goal, knowing at the end of the day that what you did was instrumental in the team's success. It is when we allow our work to consume us that I see red flags and my balance alarm bells start clanging. It is when I do not feel a company values the people within it that the rumbling deep within begins.

We must bring who we are to our work. We cannot be soulful in our personal life and soulless in our work life. I have seen this many times and it is always distressing. Truly great leaders bring soul to their work. You can see it, you can feel it, and you follow them because they are sincere. They do not divide who they are—they enhance all they do by *being* who they are. Excellence arrives because of the *who* doing the *what*. Excellence arrives because individuals are bringing value to the day in ways that leave a lasting impact on the business and the people within it. It is joyful to work with leaders this wise. It is joyful to work with anyone this wise.

Leaders are not defined by their title. They lead regardless of their salary. You will find them at all levels of an organization, any place in our world. Leaders possess a personal power that draws others to them, a soulful approach that is intangible but present no matter what they are doing. We trust people who, without reservation, bring who they are to all they do.

So recognize today that it is okay to be joyful about your work, that you can be who you are no matter where you are or what you are doing. The world, and the people around you, will be better for your courage to do so. Bring value to the day and you will find the fun just comes naturally.

CRANKY TOMATOES

Warm wind is soothing the sodden soil today, fluttering across the brilliant green of new leaves and ruffling the blooming rhododendrons. The sweet aroma of apple blossoms drifts through the air and mingles with the scent of freshly mown grass. Ahhhh . . . Spring!

My five-year-old grandson announced the other day that someone was being a "cranky tomato." When I inquired about his candid comment, he informed me that "cranky tomatoes squish themselves." Although he may not have been aware of this, his comment was very insightful. People who are cranky *do* squish themselves!

There are always those cranky tomatoes on the vine of life who inevitably tarnish the entire vine and end up with scales or scabs or rotten patches more quickly than the rest. If you think about it, when we are cranky we are spilling anger onto everyone and everything around us—but it always comes back to rest with us. We have a really crummy day when we are cranky tomatoes. The people around us have unpleasant moments in our presence, but the rest of their day is just fine. It is only our day that gets "squished." I have my cranky tomato days, and if anyone talks to me about possibilities, I spit my mushy seeds on them with delight. Only there is no delight in me that day, and by the time the sun goes down, I feel like I've been squished. We defeat ourselves by living in a cranky tomato space.

I have been teased, both literally and metaphorically, for putting sugar on my tomatoes. I like the sweet life. I like to see life as sweet, though I don't always succeed in doing so. The more I live in that sorrowful "me" place where I dwell on what isn't right or fair, the less I grow and thrive. The "sugar" I put on my tomatoes comes in a variety of forms: I grab a blanket, I lose myself in a book, I take a walk, I put extra cream in my coffee, I buy flowers at the grocery store, I allow myself to fade into the pockets of dreams. I know I don't want to be the cranky tomato on *my* vine of life. I would rather have someone slice me up and eat me for lunch than to squish myself.

May you find a way to keep the cranky tomato off your vine.

FASTING FROM FAST

The forest has gone green. Life is bursting forth more and more each day. The fronds of the maple trees spill over the branches and the new leaves seem to double in size each night. The summer birds have returned. Unlike the winter birds who sing quiet classical music in the sheltered underbrush, the summer birds turn up the rock and roll and dance from dawn till dusk. A fine dusting of golden pollen sifts to earth. On days when the spring rains and wind torment us, cascades of pink and white "snowpetals" swirl to the ground. Even on the tumultuous weather days, the air is gentler.

For several weeks I had been running through life, consumed by tasks, deadlines, and demands. Every moment of my days was filled with things that must be done and there was an ever-present ball of tension within me. I moved each day until I simply could move no more. There had not been time to be grateful for all the beauty around me and within me, no reflective time. If I sat down and closed my eyes, visions of spreadsheets, word documents, and urgent to-do lists filled my mind. My soul could not breathe, my heart could not rest, my joy could not surface. The lovely and caring universe began to poke me with messages that this was not good. My tooth broke, my back ached, my lists were incomplete, my sleep was troubled, my inspiration slipped away.

Today I decided I needed to listen. Going faster was not moving me forward. I knew I needed to "fast" from going faster. So I took a few extra minutes this morning and forced my mind to only focus on the things I loved and was grateful for. It started out slow and difficult to focus only on these things, but gradually I could feel the tension dissipate and I became aware of the warmth of the blanket, the purring cat on my lap, the vibrant beauty of spring, and the love that lived within. Like liquid gold, the joy of life slipped through me until it filled all the empty crevices and cracks, replenishing a parched spirit that had gone days without this healing, nurturing emotion. The sun peeked through the clouds, touching my toes and my heart all at once. Peace prevailed.

It is so easy to become consumed by our lives and all the things we have to do each day; so easy to forget to take the time to add richness and health to our life by slowing the pace. It just takes a few moments and a determined effort to go to the joyful places and spaces—to feel them completely. The warmth that permeated my being in those few moments balanced my perspective, renewed my energy, sparked my enthusiasm, and brought me home to the things that really matter.

Yes, I returned to the tasks and the demands of life, but they were easier. I could see the path of where to go next and feel the possibilities and loveliness of life. We often think we do not have the time to return to our core of serenity, yet it is one of the most important things we can do to smooth life's rough edges. Take the moments to remember, and feel, the joy.

WHISPER

The buds of the roses are so swollen with beauty, they surely must be about to burst forth and grace the earth with their sweet perfection and elegant presence. There is a whisper of elegance to their stems even before the blooms are born. Roses stand alone in pure beauty or sway together, caressing our eyes. They symbolize serenity at every angle in every setting. Simply stated, they are exquisite.

Whisper. What an incredible word! It is the word equivalent of a snowflake. Perfection in speech, thought, and sound. A whisper can bring a room to a standstill.

When someone whispers to you, you immediately feel privileged. You have been selected to receive secret, special information just for you to hear. And when people whisper, other people actually practice the art of listening without any conscious thought to do so. Whispered words are powerful words that leave lasting impressions. Is it because in order to deliver them and to hear them, we must be close enough to touch another human being?

One of my grandsons' favorite things to do is pull a blanket over our heads and then we whisper. There are magical tales told from a whisper, secret wisdom imparted from old to young and young to old. When we go for walks, my youngest grandson likes me to carry him through the woods. It is not because he is afraid or too tired to make the trek, but because we whisper about the birds and the trees and find special things that transform into celestial miracles simply by the hush of our voices.

Whispers float through the air and caress our senses. They turn ordinary words into vessels that deliver extraordinary messages. They live with butterfly wings and spider webs on a dew-laden day. Just whispering the word takes you to a softer place.

If we turn down the volume of our days, we will rediscover the magic and wisdom in our everyday lives.

RUBBER BOOTS

Rain tumbles from the darkening clouds in incessant torrents, leaving flowers bending low to the ground and creatures scurrying for cover. Listening to the rhythm of the watery serenade, I can tell that nature has composed a percussion solo amidst a spring concert. The air is warm, reminding us that spring is here, yet the rains continue.

It is the year of the slug. Someone in heaven forgot to shut off the hose in the Northwest. While the rains have left all plant life teeming with green, I believe the number of Prozac prescriptions in this part of the country have taken a sharp rise. A native Oregonian, I have seen rain all of my life, but no matter how acclimatized I am to this, by June, even my native bones grow weary of wet weather. I trudge through the trees, umbrella in hand, thinking about the songs and poems that depict a "walk in the rain"; I wonder if these were written by someone who lived where rain is a novelty and warm like a shower. I don't think these writers lived in the Northwest in June.

I don't really dislike rain. It has a soulful, soothing sound and sends memories of warm fires, blankets, and books through my mind. I would like to say all those memories occurred in the winter months, but I think many of them occurred in June along with wet strawberry plants and muddy knees on early mornings spent picking berries in my youth. As I walked today, I listened to the rain on the leaves and thought about how different the rain sounds as its pathway to the earth is hindered by the foliage. It is a softer but noisier sound than winter rain. Winter rains are stronger, harsher, but carry a certain silence as they drive straight to the ground without any green filters.

This observation made me think about how the rains in our lives are often similar. The harshest events fall into our world with a deepening silence that settles like cold puddles in our souls. They change who we are, define our perspectives, and bring new dimensions and understandings that we can choose to grow from or to shrivel under. The everyday rains—annoyances and difficulties in life—are noisier like the spring rains on the leaves, and though they poke and annoy us with their chatter on a daily basis, they do not leave the impact of the deeper rains. The puddles that might form from spring rains easily drift back up to the clouds and do not settle into our souls.

We protect ourselves with umbrellas—defense shields in a variety of colors and shapes known as emotions—to minimize the contact our souls have with the natural rains that move in and out of our life. There is always, however, some element of ourselves that ends up wet or cold. It is how we learn. It is how we remember to let go and feel the flow of life. It is how we are empowered to make choices about how we perceive the rains. Do we look at them with curiosity, or do we allow them to stop us from breathing in the experience? Do we continue to have faith in the sun though it is hidden from view? Do we share our umbrella with others or do we make them walk in the rain without one?

Personally, I find rubber boots to be highly valuable— on my feet and in my life. I strive to emulate their ability to keep me dry while I splash in the rain with abandon. Can I learn to live life this way? Can I find ways to walk through the puddles, to grow and share and love in spite of the days when I feel the cold and wet slip into my being? Can I keep my soul warm and embrace the rains of life? Maybe. But not in June.

BLESS-YOUS

The sky warmed the earth today as the sun made its debut. Hues of golden yellow melted into deep coral and orange, encompassing all I could see, clinging to a strand of clouds and seeming to spill into the very air. Nature was painting bliss.

I find some of the greatest epiphanies in the smallest moments of life. They catch me unawares and when they appear I am awed by the significance and the wisdom they bring with them. Everyday occurrences, everyday people, everyday moments suddenly change my perspective and offer me a different view than I had only a minute ago. I believe that we will find all that we need to know in the moments of everyday life. I believe we will find joy, love, hope, and bliss in each day if we notice it when it arrives and appreciate the magic it holds.

My four-year-old grandson had the sniffles this week, with his nose running a marathon. He assured his mother he was fine, telling her, "It's okay, Mommy. I have bless-yous in my pocket." I had to pause to catch my breath. We should all have "bless-yous" in our pockets on any given day. While my grandson simply translated tissues to bless-yous, the wisdom he spoke was inspiring. How many times every day could we pass out a "bless-you" to the people around us? The real question is, how many days would we pause long enough to remember to do so?

Life is for loving and forgiving, for graciously giving and graciously receiving. For having absolute faith in a power outside of ourselves. The most precious gifts arrive wrapped in the brown-paper packages of life. Unexpected, genuine, loving moments—magic disguised as common rhythms.

May you always seek the magic wherever you are, and may you always have "bless-yous" in your pocket.

"The highest form of wisdom is kindness."
—The Talmud

ABOUT THE AUTHOR

Heidi Levan has been writing since she was a young girl growing up on a farm outside of Portland, Oregon. As long as she can remember, she has described her observations and shared her thoughts through words—sometimes simply writing them in her head if she was not able to put her thoughts to ink. Although Heidi believes her writing talents are a gift she arrived with, she attributes her dedication to teachers who encouraged her creativity throughout her school years.

While writing is Heidi's passion, she has been a human resources director for many years. This profession has allowed her privileged insight into the commonality of all people and the opportunity to touch others with her personal and professional mission of living life with kindness, integrity, and grace.

Children, animals, and nature are Heidi's inspiration, as she finds great wisdom in them all. Home and family have always been her priority and continue to be her greatest joy. Married "forever," she and her husband have two children, four grandchildren, and six cats. Her son, Logan, illustrated *Soul Songs: Reflections of Joy in Everyday Life*.

While she can hold her own in corporate America, Heidi is still a country girl and believes simplicity and love provide the finest level of living. Her dream is to share thoughtful words that inspire curiosity and positive perspectives born from living life with love.